THE
PARADOX of
POWER

May 22, 2010

For Rose Martin,
In great respect for your
courage and integrity.
Michael
Crosby OFC.

Other Crossroad books by the author:

Solanus Casey

Can Religious Life be Prophetic?

THE PARADOX of POWER

From Control to Compassion

MICHAEL H. CROSBY

A Crossroad Book
The Crossroad Publishing Company
New York

As will be clear to the reader, my own moving "from control to compasssion" is occurring among and being influenced by my community of the Midwest Capuchin Franciscans. Because of my interaction with these dedicated men, I have been affirmed and challenged to move more deeply into the reign or power of God.

In gratitude I dedicate this book to them.

An index for this book can be found online in the "Spirituality" section of *www.michaelcrosby.net.*

Nihil Obstat
Rev. Francis Dombrowski, OFMCap., STL
Provincial Censor of Books
January 30, 2008

Very Rev. Daniel Anholzer, OFMCap.
Provincial Minister
Province of St. Joseph of the Capuchin Order
January 30, 2008

The Crossroad Publishing Company
16 Penn Plaza – 481 Eighth Avenue, Suite 1550
New York, NY 10001

Printed in the United States of America on acid-free paper

The text of this book is set in 10.5/13 Sabon. The display face is Gill Sans.

Cataloging-in-Publication Data is available from the Library of Congress

ISBN-10: 0-8245-2470-5
ISBN-13: 978-0-8245-2470-8

Contents

THE POWER CHART
TWO BASIC LIFE-PATHS: VIOLENCE OR COMPASSION

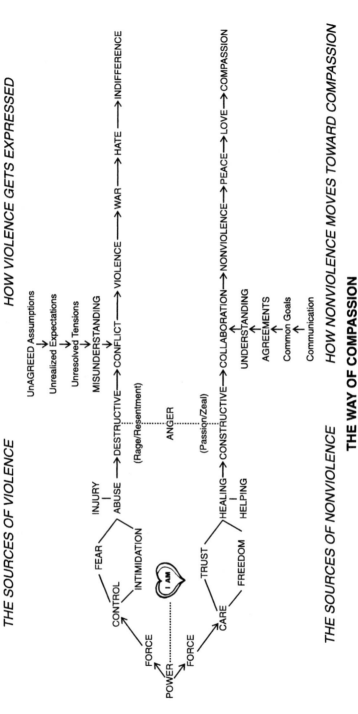

THE WAY OF VIOLENCE

THE SOURCES OF VIOLENCE   HOW VIOLENCE GETS EXPRESSED

UnAGREED Assumptions
Unrealized Expectations
Unresolved Tensions
MISUNDERSTANDING

VIOLENCE → WAR → HATE → INDIFFERENCE

DESTRUCTIVE → CONFLICT →
(Rage/Resentment)

ANGER

(Passion/Zeal)
CONSTRUCTIVE → COLLABORATION → NONVIOLENCE → PEACE → LOVE → COMPASSION

UNDERSTANDING
AGREEMENTS
Common Goals
Communication

INJURY
ABUSE
FEAR
INTIMIDATION
CONTROL
FORCE
I AM
POWER
FORCE
TRUST
CARE
FREEDOM
HEALING
HELPING

THE SOURCES OF NONVIOLENCE   HOW NONVIOLENCE MOVES TOWARD COMPASSION

THE WAY OF COMPASSION

Summary of Key Concepts in the Power Chart

Everything regarding violence, nonviolence, and compassion begins with *power*. Power is the ability to influence. It can be positive or negative. Force is directed power. It too can be positive or negative. When power is expressed as a positive force, via affirmation and correction, it is expressive of CARE. When power becomes a negative force, via exploitation, manipulation, or domination (or lack of CARE), it is experienced as CONTROL. Abuse is any kind of behavior (influence) that one person, group, or institution uses to control another through fear and intimidation. Healing, which differs from a cure, reflects the restoration of the whole. Diagram and explanation by Michael Crosby, OFMCap. © 2009 Michael Crosby.

Working Definitions

Abuse: Any use of control exercised through fear and intimidation.

Care: The positive use of power. That which empowers or energizes.

Compassion: Empowering care made universal.

Control: The negative use of power. That which overpowers or de-energizes.

Health: Wellness in any body.

Indifference: The ultimate lack of care.

Nonviolence: Any directed power strategically exercised with a goal of minimizing injury and bringing about positive change.

Power: The ability to influence. Energy.

Terrorism: The intentional threat or effort to use violence against civilians.

Violence: Any (un)intentional power or force that inflicts injury.

Preface

The Origin of This Book

For almost twenty years I have led workshops on the positive and negative uses of power. People have said these helped them move from power's negative expression in control and violence to show its positive face in care and compassion. Invariably, at every workshop people ask me if any of my books contain what I've shared verbally. Until now, I have not been able to give them anything. This is not because people have not tried to make it happen!

In 1995 Michael Leach, then the publisher at Crossroad, asked me to communicate my ideas in print form. He even transcribed tapes from a workshop he had attended. There I spoke on the polarities of power that can be found on the Power Chart on page 8 of this book. He did a fine job. I kept his transcript in a file. Meanwhile I continued giving the workshops around the Power Chart throughout the world. Then, ten years after Michael transcribed the workshop, a woman who had attended a weekend on the subject in Nova Scotia a year earlier surprised me with an unsolicited transcript of what I had said. These transcripts form the basis of this book.

That the notion of power itself is paradoxical is evident from an incident that took place as I began writing this book. I mentioned my effort to someone whom I consider to be a "power person" in the sense that she is very influential. Her response made me realize, more than ever, the need for something like the approach to power I offer here. She said: "Society is crying for something like this. It is so critical to understand why so many people in our world, especially us in this country, are addicted to power. This need to control is destroying ourselves, those around us, and our world."

Why did she assume a book on power would revolve around issues of control? I think that the reason for her response can be found in the fact that, for most of us living in a political economy like the United States and a faith community like the Roman Catholic Church, issues related to the negative use of power, such as control or domination, have come to define our mode of being and functioning. Consequently, we find ourselves very ambivalent regarding the notion of power and whether we "want" power, assuming that we can never be powerless, when we really mean giving up the need to control, which is the negative use of power.

Confusion over the idea of power is not limited only to those of us who live in cultures and structures where the abuses of power are often unrecognized, unacknowledged, and even denied (and, therefore, can be much more destructive). If phenomenologists like the social critic Michel Foucault are right, this ambivalence seems to be something that arises from our multivalent experiences of power in its various forms. Because of some negative experiences of power around the dynamics of control, we often fail to realize the universe itself exists because of positive power — which can be harnessed for the good of others and ourselves. Foucault wrote:

> What makes power hold good, what makes it accepted, is simply the fact that it doesn't only weigh on us as a force that says no, but that it traverses and produces things, it induces pleasure, forms knowledge, and produces discourse. It needs to be considered as a productive network that runs through the whole social body, much more than as a negative instance whose function is repression.[1]

Despite the fact that Foucault shows, at least in this part of his discussion of power, that the "good outweighs the bad" when we think of power, why is it that we so often identify power with its negative expression rather than its positive face? I think a lot can be traced to the culture and institutions in which we have been raised.

As citizens, we have defined our national identity and destiny almost since our nation's inception around "Manifest Destiny": we are chosen to be the world's governor. As I was finishing this book a Gallup Poll appeared with some questions related to U.S. military power around the world. Sixty-one percent of the respondents felt "that it is important for the United States to be No. 1 in the world militarily" while 38 percent said it was "not important as long as the U.S. is among the leading military powers."[2] When we read books on the lobbying and influence of corporations on our political processes, we find it hard to believe that corruption around the influence of money has been able to undermine the political processes of people-power to such a degree — until we have another scandal, like that involving lobbyist Jack Abramoff, which was exposed as I began to write this book. "How can this be?" we ask of our own government officials.

In the Roman Church we seem quite content in our pews until the press reveals that some of our priests and not a few of our bishops have abused their power because of their ability to maintain their corporate control over the whole church apparatus. When it takes the form of pedophilia and the cover-up in the United States or collaboration with the Communist government by many clerics at all levels in Poland, we still seem shocked at such power abuses. In such cases it seems our clerics appear more like the scribes and Pharisees of Matthew's Gospel than the One who stated that their way of power was not to be like that of the authorities around them (see Matt. 20:25).

This book will address the issue of power as control and how control, used negatively, can be found at the heart of so many conflicts and violence in, among, and around us in ways that overpower and de-energize others in our spheres of influence. It will also show how power manifests itself as a positive and creative force that heals and constructs healthy relationships, marriages, and families, as well as successful organizations such as corporations, churches, and even nations. When this occurs, it becomes an energizing and empowering force for good.

Beneath it all and at the heart of it all I want to show that the God in whom I believe, who, I am convinced, is the energy or force behind all power in the universe, is within me and every reader of this book — as well as every person and everything in the universe. As a Christian, I want to promote a vision of the Trinitarian God whose rule or way of relating must be at the core of all relationships in our world, be they personal, communal, or collective. This triune reality is realized in the fact that the three unique "I ams" can claim equality in the Godhead only to the degree that all have equal access to full resources of their commonwealth and, indeed, exist to ensure that equality of access, not just for their own "I am" but, equally for those with whom they are in relationship. It is this all-powerful God, revealed in the power of the Gospel of Jesus Christ and in whose Spirit/Energy we live, move, and have our being individually, communally, and collectively that impels me to write these words.

How to Read This Book

When I give workshops I combine words written on a board with my verbal expressions, and of course there is interaction with the participants. Consequently, when I give such talks on the topic of power, my audiences are more easily able to make the kind of connections they find helpful. When I point to parts of the Power Chart and make connections, especially from my own experiences, they are able to take what is most personal to me and find its application in their own lives. I strongly suggest that readers have handy the Power Chart while reading the chapters of this book as a useful aid to the flow of the material presented. At the same time, please keep in mind that, like in workshops, sometimes ideas and thoughts are shared or examples given that may not be fully fleshed out, so "dialogue" with me as you read. Or better, read this with others.

This book can be read in two ways. The first would be to follow the chapters as I offer them. This builds on the definition of power as "the ability to influence." It then outlines the negative expressions of power, moving in increasingly negative dynamics from control and violence to indifference. The second half of the book addresses the power dynamics that occur when they are positively manifested. Here we find ways of moving from care to compassion that create communities of trust and freedom and empower us to learn the way of nonviolence, peace, and love.

A second way of reading this book involves taking each of the concepts on the top part of the Power Chart and contrast them with their alternative expression of parallel power that is found beneath it, on the bottom part of the chart. If this would be done, the reader would begin by reading the chapters about the grounding of negative power in control and then the chapters on its positive foundation in care. This would then lead to reflection on how control dynamics end up in abusive relationships that are defined via fear and intimidation or, as the parallel on the bottom of the chart shows, in healthy relationships grounded in freedom and trust. In this top/bottom approach it would be clear, by the end of the book, that compassion is the antidote to indifference, much like the parallels described in the "Peace Prayer" attributed to St. Francis: "where there is injury, pardon; where there is hatred, love," and so on.

If you choose to read the chapters sequentially, you will follow the model I use in my workshops. However, since the message I am sharing also wants to emphasize using power in a positive direction to overcome negative manifestations of power, it may be more helpful to use the second method. Whatever approach is taken, it is my hope that you will be enlightened to move from control to care, from violence to nonviolence, and from any kind of indifference to the pain in, among, and around you to the kind of compassion that will contribute to the promise of a new kind of social order for our world and all who inhabit it.

In many ways, given the noting of moving from control to compassion, The Power Chart assumes we are on a journey. In contemporary spiritual language, this is called "conversion." While I use contemporary language to describe these dynamics, this process of conversion involves moving from what is negative (i.e., sin) to what is positive (i.e., grace). It involves moving from death to life, darkness to light, the tomb to resurrection, sickness to health, from what overpowers and de-energizes us and others to ways of relating that empower and energize our inter-actions. It is meant to help heal rather than continue the hurts. In other words, it outlines the dynamics of letting God's energy (which we call Spirit) define who we are and how we relate to everyone and everything.

I want to thank all those who have walked with me and who continue to be present to me on my own journey of moving from control to compassion.

To Michael Leach (who first suggested I flesh out my thoughts in writing), to Liz Wisniewski (my office manager), to Eugene LeBoeuf (who put form to the Power Chart), and, finally, to the various editors who have helped put this book in its present form, I offer my deepest thanks for enabling this book finally see the light of day.

Chapter One

Power as the Force of Energy
at the Heart of All That Is

It is a dictum that something cannot be true in one area of life and false in another. This realization has been especially relevant in issues related to science and religion. Something cannot be true in science and be denied in religion if that religion is to "make sense." Since science, by definition, deals with that which is observable (and, therefore, factually verifiable) while religion involves that which is beyond measurability, it becomes especially important to realize that something cannot be true in religion if it is denied by science. While science might not be able to explain the mysteries of religion, the mysteries themselves must make sense.

In its special millennial edition, January 1, 2000, the *Wall Street Journal* interviewed a host of experts in various fields, asking them about their thoughts regarding the future in disciplines in which they excelled. One of these was Edward O. Wilson of Harvard University whose book *On Human Nature* received a Pulitzer Prize.

The *Journal* asked him a question that directly addresses the issue of science and religion: "How can religion possibly survive what science is doing?" After noting that the expansion of human knowledge with science and technology has rendered "religious belief less and less tenable, more and more difficult to justify and argue logically," Dr. Wilson uttered a sentence that has challenged my thinking as a priest and theologian in the Roman Catholic Church: "The more we understand from science about the way the world really works, all the way from subatomic particles up to the mind and on to the cosmos, the more difficult it is to base spirituality on our ancient mythologies."[1]

We cannot come to a learning about power in the field of science, whether it be physics or cosmology, only to have that undermined by the way religion addresses power and, more importantly, witnesses to a way of relating around power. The two areas of science and religion cannot have mutually exclusive ways of addressing the phenomenon of power if either is to be considered healthy and authentic. The same holds true of phenomenology or sociology that deal with relationships, whether reading Michel Foucault, who finds all relationships involving some kind of power, or sociologist Anthony Giddens, who has claimed that power "is a feature of every human interaction"[2] and that even the most innocent-appearing interaction between two people "is a relation of power, to which the participants may bring unequal resources"[3] that can aid or undermine people's lives.

Probably the greatest scientific learning I have received in the last decade involves my awareness of the connectedness of everything in the universe. This has led me to realize that the heart of reality is more than can be seen, or as an article in the *Wall Street Journal* noted of quantum theory: "quantum advances are making conventional understanding about what exists and what is real start 'to melt away.'" Indeed, the article showed, not only what appears as the greatest is the least but also the micro is the macro.[4] This awareness has convinced me of the need to work toward ever greater forms of mutuality, solidarity, and connectedness in my life and surroundings. It is an awareness that the same vibrational energy within me exists in all of creation.

At the same time, and in a way that parallels what I am continually learning from science, my greatest faith-learning has come from my resulting faith-based conviction that the Trinitarian God, the Creating Force of the Universe from the beginning of time (if that notion still can be accepted) until all is consummated (in that love which is God), must be the model of all connectedness in the universe. This has forced me to look at my own spirituality through another lens. It has deeply affected my awareness of the power involved in my relationships, especially with those where I live and among whom I minister. It has also made me even more committed to challenge those structures that justify their unequal power relationships by an appeal to a god of an earlier scientific vision of the world but who no longer makes sense and, to that degree, is simply un-believe-able or in-cred-ible.

In fine, on the one hand I find that power in the form of relational energy constitutes our very identity as an "I am" made in the image of God and drives our universe as well; on the other, I can only believe in a Trinitarian God whose relational energy is the power and whose symmetrical or equal power-relationships constitute what we, as well as our universe, must be. The implications of this conviction and belief serve as the operating metaphor for this book and the Power Chart around which it revolves. This first chapter offers more background for this conviction and belief.

Power as Relational Energy

Whether from scientific knowledge or religious beliefs, it is becoming increasingly clear that all life is about relationships, and all relationships involve a kind of connectedness around energy forces. Following the conclusion of Dr. Wilson above regarding the need to make sure our religious belief (and actions) reflect what we are learning about power from physics, phenomenology, and cosmology, we keep returning to similar understandings of power.

When we consider the world of matter from the viewpoint of a physicist (at its most micro-level), a cosmologist (at its most macro-level), or a biologist (who investigates the world of cells, organisms, and living systems and finds basic interconnections), we find that everything in the universe is not what we see (i.e., observable matter) but the result of what is not seen; everything that is, is what it is because of relationships that emanate from forces of energy or power. What scientists have known for a century has now become common knowledge through everything from awareness of DNA to computer chips.

The post-Einstein age has made us deeply aware of the connectedness of all things and everyone in such a way that everything that appears as matter is, in truth, forms of energy expressed in connectedness. This book is a form of matter. Your hand that holds the book is another form of matter — along with your eyes that read the words (which may be helped by glasses, which are matter in another expression). All matter is composed of atoms that are connected. But these atoms are what they are because of the subatomic particles that constitute their existence via the neutrons and the protons that are in relationship to each other. And these core ingredients of the atom are what they are because of certain entities called quarks which are really packets of energy itself. So at the heart of all matter we find energy. All matter is really energy. This energy is power; this power is what makes us all connected; it is relationality itself.

At the micro-level of the world of the smallest cell we find the cell of the macro-world of our universe. Indeed, we exist because we are part of one great energy field. When we study cellular biology we find parallel learnings in social biology and cosmology: the outer is the inner, and the inner is the outer. I am my universe. We can say that every part of the universe contains the entire universe; thus all must "work together" for the good of the whole. As the Chinese saying has it: "Here is everywhere. You just have to find it." At the same time, for us who say: "I believe in God, the Almighty [i.e., the all-powerful], the Creator of the world," we find God to be the Spirit or Energy that holds together and empowers the micro- and macro-levels of our universe. This God has been revealed to us Christians as Trinitarian in nature; thus in God there can be no subordination, for such would be an abuse of power among God's triadic community. More specifically, as a Franciscan, I believe that God so loves the world that the "I am" of the Trinity we call "Word" moved from being pure spirit to matter, to be incarnated in a form of matter that this One had already made from the beginning. So all matter comes together in the Cosmic Christ, who maintains "first place," or primacy, in everything that has ever existed, exists now, or will ever exist.[5] Furthermore, I believe that the fullness of this Christ exists in that "body called church" and that, consequently, the church's functioning must ultimately reveal what Christ came to proclaim and to bring about: the reign or power of the Trinity at the heart of all reality. When we consider the "kingdom of God" (really the "kin-dom" or new relationality) that Jesus revealed, we realize that it was such a threat because it challenged the assumptions and presumptions of the "powers and principalities" that dominated the people of his day. The Trinity subverts all untrinitarian relationships.

When we move from the scientific world to the world of psychology, we find relationality and power dynamics have defined our identity with ourselves as well as our connectedness with others. A very active child is often described as a bundle of energy. This image is truer than we might imagine. Actually each one of us in our "I am" is a bundle of energies. These underlying powers or forces within us enable us to be the unique "I am" that we are: unique icons or images of that original "I am" we call God. These divinely grounded energies that define our individual persons are represented as the energies of our heart. As people of "The Book," we know that the heart represents our "I am"; thus I am to love God with my whole heart; I am to love my self and I am to love my neighbor wholeheartedly or with all my energy or power. Indeed, my uniqueness as a human is summarized in the statement: "I am." I am the summary of my thoughts, my feelings, and my actions. Traditionally and in the scriptures, our "I am" has been identified with the image of the heart. Thus we have "thoughts" of the heart, heartfelt emotions, and sayings like "your actions tell where you heart is." Thus we place the heart with its "I am," along with our thinking, feeling, and acting, parallel to power on our chart.[6] At the same time my "I am" represents my core identifier, my *self*.

I may think that I am an individual person inhabiting a body in a certain space and time. But within my "self" exists a very complex person who has an inner and an outer dimension. My inner self or "I am" is my true self. It is an amalgam of the energies of the universe that give me my identity. At the same time, since I am born into this world, I have an outer dimension insofar as my "I am" is in relationship with others. By definition as a "self," I am in relationship with other "I ams." Indeed, as Nel Noddings writes, the " 'best self' is a relational entity."[7] All life involves relationships, and all relationships, especially those of significance, involve power or ways we relate to or influence each other as individuals, groups, and collective entities.

We have been divinely constituted so that, from conception to death, each of us is connected to other persons beyond our unique "I ams" or ourselves. Each of these persons has been created to realize his or her core energies as well. However, because we exist only in relationships we can say that each person has a basic energy or need to be a unique "I am," and to be affirmed in that uniqueness. Each person also needs to be accepted as "good enough" by others; to be free as unique persons and, in relationship, to be free of others' efforts to control and free of those dynamics that might deny one's freedom. Finally, each person needs not just to love, but to be loved as well. We want to resonate one with the other.

In terms of the energy called love, it actually becomes the summary of all energies insofar as the first image we get from those voices outside our "I am" (if they represent healthy persons) is: "I am lovable." As we continue to mature it will be this energy, love, that will come to dominate our "I am" if we commit ourselves to a life of care. This care will define our "belonging." Or its opposite, control, will undermine the integrity of who "I am." The task of life is to find a way to move from the negative forms of power in and around us to reclaim that "original goodness" that dwells deep within, which is what we believers call "the reign [the power] of God." This invites us to move from what Nel Noddings calls the "pathologies of care" into authentic care.[8]

A deeper examination of who we are and among whom we relate indicates that we are continually influenced to live one way by nature (harmoniously) and another way by much of our nurturing (competitively). Consequently we live in two worlds: an inner world from which we must live empowered and an outer world that can easily overpower us. When I live in my inner world of equal power with others, I live in a caring environment; I am free and trusting and show similar care to others. However, I too often find myself in a negative environment where I feel overpowered and de-energized by others who are trying to control me or others whom I feel I need to please. The goal of life is to find a way, in the context of all those outer voices and forces they represent, to listen to our inner voice and become the "I am" we have been created to be. The process of living is ordered to this goal in life. Best-selling author Sue Monk Kidd describes how it happened to her:

> One day driving down the street, I asked myself, "Sue Monk Kidd, who are you?" And right away the obvious answers came. "You are Bob and Ann's mother, Sandy's wife, Leah and Ridley's daughter, a writer.... All nice things." Then I asked myself. "So if all those roles were stripped away, *then* who would you be?" The question jolted me. It brought me to stand before the bare mystery of my own being. Was there something deeper at the very core of me that was purely and truly my "I"?
>
> I came to believe ... that our true identity goes beyond the outer roles we play. It transcends the ego. I came to understand that there is an Authentic "I" within — an "I-Am."[9]

Power as Relational Energy
Connecting Us to All in the Universe

All relationships, at every level of life, involve dynamics on a continuum from mutually positive and more-or-less equal power dynamics to negative or unequal power dynamics. Consequently, the manifestation of power will demonstrate degrees of more or less functional relationships, resulting in equilibrium, or dysfunctional and destructive dynamics, resulting in imbalance and unequal power relationships.

Hannah Arendt insisted that there could be no power except in relationship. For her, power is "the human ability ... to act in concert."[10] As such our identity, our "I am," actually arises *from* the relationship; we do not bring our "I am" *to* the relationship. Without relationship, humans are powerless.

Human beings are totally powerless at birth; we survive because of the care of others. The authors of *The Dynamics of Power* observe:

> The roots of power are imbedded in the human infant's condition of helplessness experienced at birth and for some time thereafter. We are all born utterly powerless, entirely dependent upon the good will and loving care of human caretakers.... The state of powerlessness into which we are born, a condition which must be endured over an extended time frame, conditions our emergent need for power as human development unfolds....

Powerlessness is the experiential ground from which emerges the earliest sense of self. It is powerlessness which gives birth to our need for power: to control our hands, to make our legs move as we will, to control our bodies and all their functions, to speak our thoughts and have them listened to, to go where we will, to chart our own path according to our inner promptings, to control our own lives and destinies as best we can. It is the profound condition of helplessness in infancy, lasting over many months, which shapes our destiny to become in turn shapers of the social landscape in which we flourish.[11]

Something interesting happens relative to the early dynamics of control and the way we try to gain mastery over our bodies and their functions. It translates into our relationships, and we find ourselves exhibiting dynamics that try to control others rather than show them genuine care and regard.

When I engage other persons beyond myself, I create various groupings or communities. These will be affected by, and influenced by, my energies. The ways in which we connect, relate, and use power — whether in ways that overpower (conditioned control) or empower (unconditional care) — is critical to our relationships at all levels of life: intrapersonal (how "I am" in relationship to my "self"); interpersonal (family and friends, coworkers and neighbors); and the social arrangements that determine who has power and who does not. Care rather than control ideally defines the way of relating at all levels.

For instance, at the intrapersonal level, when care defines who "I am," I have been able to integrate my vision of myself as one who cares with my actual practice of care toward myself and others. At the interpersonal level, the way I care for others comes from a genuine care for them free of negative power dynamics (such as manipulation or domination, coercion or exploitation). In this way of relating I empower myself to be an ethical or caring person or, as Nel Noddings writes, in recognizing my fundamental situation of being in relatedness I find myself naturally connected to others. In the process I become reconnected "through the other to myself. As I care for others and am cared for by them, I become able to care for myself."[12]

Because energy is at the heart of all matter, when relationships at any level of life are empowering, they will energize those involved in the relationship. However, when they are negative in their expression, they will be a force that de-energizes those who are involved and will undermine the health of the relationship itself.

Power as the Ability to Influence Others
in Our Relationships

Despite all the theories about power in its human and divine expressions, I think it can be safely stated that most of us are conflicted about the notion of power itself.

I define power as "the ability to influence." As I begin my workshops, I try to make my audience aware of the fact that there are two kinds of power being exercised in all relationships. I begin by asking: "How many of you *want power?*" Possibly because it is a direct and concise question, people's first reaction is to feel confused. Depending on the group, many or few will raise their hand. Then I ask: "How many of you *don't want power?*" Again, many or few will raise their hand, depending on the makeup of the group. For instance, if it is a group of business people, the majority will say they want power. Politicians will be conflicted because they don't want to admit publicly that they may be operating more from self-interest than the public good. The least likely to raise their hands will be those self-identified as religious, since their self-image is to be caring and nurturing.

Then I'll say: "It looks like a good number of you don't know what you want," which always gets a laugh and relaxes the group. I proceed to give the first of three definitions that have changed the way I relate and respond to others: it is my definition of power itself. For me, power is simply "the ability to influence." Power can be exercised by myself or another. That "other" can be an individual, a group, an institution, or a force beyond human dynamics, such as the force of a hurricane or the energy of a waterfall.

Upon sharing with groups my definition of power, I write it on a board. Then I ask my earlier question again: "So now that you real-ize that power is simply 'the ability to influence,' how many of you *want* power?" Everyone's hand immediately goes up. "So," I ask various people, "Who do you want to influence?" Responses vary. "My wife and kids." "A certain group that I want to be part of." "The president and Congress." "The advertisers who always have more influence over my kids than I do." "My boss." "My grandkids." When I give the workshop to Catholics, I invariably hear the older ones say, "I want to influence my kids (or grandchildren) to go to church."

An article in the *Wall Street Journal* discussed what it called "Leading from Below." The basic argument revolved around the fact that, al-though the "importance of leadership from the top is firmly embedded in corporate culture," studies of managers revealed that the most successful ones focus "on influence, not control." Indeed, the way they influenced others "below" them, through respect and collaboration, spelled the difference between their being successful or not, powerful or not.[13]

All life is interrelational. Being in relationship and having power address our basic need to be. Why? Because "to be" is "to be with." I cannot say "I am" except in relationship. All relationships, especially significant relationships, involve not only power, but also directed power or force in the form of influence, for good and harm. How I influence others in relationships and how I am influenced by others will be a force for good or harm in the world. At the same time, my world will be a force for harm in my life. All directed power represents a force of some kind, and as such it will be a force that energizes or de-energizes those involved. Relationships can be healthy or hurtful, constructive or destructive, collaborative or conflictual, nonviolent or violent. They can be peaceful, loving, and compassionate, or they can be warring, hateful, and lead to a kind of indifference that is the opposite of care.

The Interconnectedness of Power at All Levels

What are the objects in our search for power? A survey of first-year collegians at a major university discovered that the three things students wanted most as a result of their education were power, money, and a reputation. They learned this well from their parents: the main goals of Americans revolve around dynamics related to power itself (how we can influence others), property issues, and prestige or image issues. A fourth is a *sine qua non*: sex. All of these objects of power are important in our lives and relationships; they are good in themselves. Not only that, they are basic needs. We all need power. We all must survive. We all need a good name. We need to perpetuate our species.

While these four objectives involving power dynamics have value in themselves, the way we relate to one another as individuals, groups, and institutions (from nations to religions) as we reach toward these goals will involve positive and negative power dynamics. The dynamics come into play at the personal and group levels, but also at the heart of global relationships. When global relationships are structured negatively, we find disorder, disequilibrium, and dysfunctionality between nations. When institutions are organized and structured around unequal power dynamics, in which one group overpowers another or ensures its access to resources at the expense of others, the result is what I call "isms" based on unequal power relationships. "Isms" have an overwhelming influence on how power itself will become a force for harm in our increasingly interconnected family of nations.

"Isms" are institutionally ordered relationships that ensure unequal relationships of power among observably different groups. For instance, historically unequal power relationships between women and men result in "sexism." When white people benefit systemically at the expense of people of other races, it is called "racism." The results of "nationalism," "tribalism," and "ethnocentrism" are found in conflicts and wars that never seem to end.

Society is defined by these and various other "isms" that reveal unequal power relationships among people that are institutionalized and ideologically justified: classism, clericalism, ageism, and heterosexism are a few that come to mind. Such "isms" breed other "isms" that sustain structured inequity in the allocation of resources: consumerism, materialism, economic imperialism, militarism. Indeed, as I was writing this book, I read of a new "ism" called "petrolism," coined by Thomas L. Friedman.[14]

When these unequal power relationships among persons and societal resources result from historical situations, they can easily be legitimized (i.e., set in law) in political and cultural milieus and canonized in religious laws. When this occurs, the development of ideological justification for the institutions to maintain the "isms" increases the benefit to the group in control.

"Ideology" has various meanings that can be positive or negative. Sandra Polaski has shown, however, that in either case "the articulation of an ideology *is* a power claim."[15] As such it merits special attention. It can simply refer to a way of thinking that guides a specific person's behavior. "Ideology" also refers to certain philosophies, such as individualism or relativism, that characterize a group's thought processes. However, when I use the term "ideology" in this book I do so negatively or pejoratively insofar as it refers to the way of thinking various groups develop and express regarding the social arrangements and ordering (i.e., the "isms") that take place in their institutions in ways that benefit them at the expense of others. According to Anthony Giddens, ideology represents the power of some social actors (the powerful) to make their own interests appear to be universal interests, to be normal, or to be the only way imaginable.[16] Consequently and often unconsciously, those who benefit from the unequal power relationship will deny that the ideologies exist. That is because they do not experience "reality" as anything but that which benefits them. Those who feel the brunt of the disparity in the relationship experience its negative effects in more or less alienating ways. We have only to think of the graphic images of Hurricane Katrina in 2005 as a classic example of disparities in power that exposed the "reality" gulf between whites and minorities.

When we consider Jesus and his proclamation of the Gospel, we find that he challenged the underlying ideologies of the key institutions of his day: the leaders of his own religion and the leaders of the empire.

It's to this conflict over his power (or his ability to influence) that we now turn.

Chapter Two

God's Power
at the Heart of the World:
The Gospel of Power

It will be shown later, following the Power Chart, that conflicts arise from two key sources: (1) the desire or need for control on the part of some body or some group; and (2) misunderstandings among various parties in a relationship. Whether for reasons of control or because of basic misunderstandings about unrealized expectations on the part of Jesus' co-religionists, both the Synoptic versions as well as the Johannine story make it clear: conflict is central to the life and death of Jesus.

The ultimate conflict between Jesus and his adversaries involved competing power claims, as is evident in the verbal altercation between Jesus and the "chief priests and the elders of the people." This occurred when he entered the Jerusalem temple after first using his power to free it from those "who were selling and buying in the temple" (Matt. 21:12; par. Mark 11:27–33):

> "By what authority [*exousia*] are you doing these things, and who gave you this authority [*exousia*]?" Jesus said to them, "I will also ask you one question; if you tell me the answer, then I will also tell you by what authority [*exousia*] I do these things. Did the baptism of John come from heaven, or was it of human origin?" And they argued with one another, "If we say, 'From heaven,' he will say to us, 'Why then did you not believe him?' But if we say, 'Of human origin,' we are afraid of the crowd; for all regard John as a prophet." So they answered Jesus, "We do not know." And he said to them, "Neither will I tell you by what authority [*exousia*] I am doing these things" (Matt. 21:23–27).

The result of this confrontation, Matthew tells us, is the decision of the authorities to get rid of Jesus once and for all: "They wanted to arrest him, but they feared the crowds, because they regarded him as a prophet" (Matt. 21:46).

Clearly, the Gospel story of Jesus revolves around power. This power involves relational dynamics that are increasingly conflictual to the point that the religious leaders are portrayed as indifferent to anything but the preservation of their control. Scholar Bruce Malina studied the anthropological dynamics that defined relationships in the culture in which Jesus lived. He identified a triad of "boundary markers" among people that revolved around power, sexual status, and religion. *Power* need not always be defined as a physical force, but it always represents "the ability to exercise control over the behavior of others." *Sexual status* (or roles) refers to "the sets of duties and rights — what you ought to do and what others ought do to or for you" that derive from sexual differentiation. Finally, *religion* involves the "attitude and behavior one is expected to follow relative to those who control one's existence."[1]

As a religious reformer, Jesus came into conflict with religious authorities intent on maintaining their control. In turn, they feared losing their power, in the form of control, because they might be replaced by those in Rome who had greater power and who felt their exercise of power was legitimated by their own religion. Such conflicts over power and, especially power that seemed religiously sanctioned, bring us to four approaches to this theme as found in the Christian scriptures.

Mark's Gospel: The Confrontation of Jesus' Power with That of the Authorities

The Gospel stories of Jesus and his message and his impact on the "power players" in his world cannot be interpreted apart from the dynamics of power. This is clear from the Gospel according to Mark, the first of the four Gospel stories of Jesus to be written.[2] While the author, along with almost all the other authors in the New Testament, uses the word *dúnamis* for power, Mark's use of another word for power has special meaning in his Gospel. This word is *exousia*.

In her sociopolitical reading of Mark's Gospel, *Freedom as Liberating Power,* Anne Dawson finds that Mark's choice of the word *exousia* (power or authority) in relation to Jesus was the Gospel writer's way of placing Jesus in opposition to the imperial system and its ideology of Pax Romana. As such, from the margins of a small Jewish outpost whose religious leaders had assimilated to imperial ways, the coming of Jesus threatened the existing global order as well as its religious underpinnings.

Finding the origin of *exousia* in the verb *exestin,* meaning "it is free,"[3] Dawson defines *exousia* as the "freedom to act." In light of its origin and what I have written thus far, I would define *exousia* as "being empowered." She writes: "Mark's Gospel portrays a picture of Jesus who acted with ἐξουσία and who called on his followers to act likewise. In doing so, Jesus in fact subverted the notion of freedom that Rome proclaimed."[4]

The "freedom to act" that defined all relationships under Roman rule meant submitting to its control in order to bring about security among its citizens and subjects. This Pax Romana was enshrined in various documents, including the *Res Gestae,* which was an inscription related to the power of the divinely anointed one, Augustus, who ruled "the world" at the time of Jesus as its "Savior." It was intended to convey a universal message or Gospel for a universal audience. The message was simply that both Augustus and the people were free because they had been empowered to act. It stressed the power and authority of Augustus that had brought about universal freedom, victory, peace, mercy, honor, justice, faith, and right worship. According to Dawson this "world behind the text" of Mark must be understood if the Gospel of Mark itself is to be fully appreciated. She concludes:

> In particular the linguistic codes and symbols evident in the texts of the *Res Gestae* inscription pointed to the perspective regarding the ideology of power that prevailed during the reign of Augustus. The subsequent promulgation of this ideology of power through the medium of the *Res Gestae* text inscribed on monuments throughout the Roman occupied world, was a legacy that Augustus bequeathed to future generations. This was a legacy of an ideology of power to which subsequent emperors of the Roman Empire subscribed. It was within the climate of this socio-political world that the message of Jesus was also proclaimed.[5]

Whether it was by taking notions traditionally identified with Augustus, such as "Son of Man" or "Lord" (*kyrios*) and then applying them to Jesus, the author of Mark seems to have clearly wanted to proclaim Jesus as proclaiming another "Gospel" than that identified with and sustaining the power of the ruling authorities. This becomes even clearer, Dawson insists, if we examine the structure of Mark's narrative:

> Having established the ἐξουσία of Jesus and the disciples in the first half of the Gospel narrative (Mark 1:1–8:30), the narrator, in the second half, then relates how the ἐξουσία of both Jesus and the disciples was tested to the ultimate degree (Mark 9:2–16:8). Again

the word ἐξουσία is a key term in this section of the narrative, where it is found in two episodes that the narrator records. The first is in reference to Jesus in Mark 11:1, 27–33 where Jesus comes into direct confrontation with the "authorities" in Jerusalem. The second is in reference to the disciples by way of a parable that Jesus relates (Mark 11:33–34).[6]

"In selecting ἐξουσία as a key term in his 'narrative,' the author of Mark's Gospel wanted to draw the attention of his audience to the concept of the *praxis* of Christian freedom," Dawson writes. This "power to be and to act" on the part of Jesus and his disciples sets them up against the established power of the religious and civil leaders around them. It is little wonder then, that Mark would have Jesus actually identify the "kingdom" with power itself (Mark 9:1).[7]

Matthew's Gospel: The Empowering of Jesus' Disciples for "the Whole World"

The Gospel of Matthew parallels and expands Mark's use of the word *exousia*. When we set the word in the context of the whole Gospel and examine the confrontation of Jesus with the authorities, especially those of his own religion who took orders from Rome rather than from the Jewish people, the conflict over power between Jesus and his religious and civil authorities is even clearer. With its addition of a nativity narrative, Matthew's Gospel stresses this conflict from the very beginning.

The surrogate of Augustus in Palestine was Herod, who presided as "King of the Jews" (46 B.C.E.–4 B.C.E.) at the time that Jesus, another "King of the Jews," was reportedly born. When the *magoi* come seeking the Messiah they find their way to Herod. There they ask: "Where is the child who has been born king of the Jews?" Not only does Matthew make their question a direct challenge to Herod's authority as king; they indicate that it is to this one that they are prepared "to pay him homage" (Matt. 2:2).

Herod's reaction is fascinating: "When King Herod heard this, he was frightened, and all Jerusalem with him" (Matt. 2:3). *All* Jerusalem with him? Who are these "all" in Jerusalem? They could not be the *hoi poloi*, the average Jews who disdained Herod and saw him as a puppet of Rome; they could only be the "chief priests and scribes of the people," who themselves would be threatened if anything happened to usurp Herod's claims to power (see Matt. 2:4).

Later, in his public ministry, Jesus proclaimed: "Repent, for the kingdom of heaven has come near" (Matt. 4:17). From here he calls his own disciples (Matt. 4:18–22) as he goes "throughout Galilee, teaching in their synagogues and proclaiming the good news of the kingdom and curing every disease and every sickness among the people" (Matt. 4:23; see also 9:35).

Building on Mark's original approach, Matthew portrays Jesus' proclamation of the Gospel as defined by *exousia*. Matthew incorporates eight of the nine times Mark uses the word; his two unique usages refer to the way Matthew envisions the power of God at work in Jesus and the Apostles as continuing in time when "two or three" gather "in the name," or power, of its source.

In all, *exousia* appears ten times in Matthew, first at the end of the Sermon on the Mount: "Now when Jesus had finished saying these things, the crowds were astounded at his teaching, for he taught them as one having *exousia,* and not as their scribes" (Matt. 7:28–29). He next uses it when the centurion acknowledges Jesus' authority as greater than his (see 8:9). When Jesus heals a paralyzed man and forgives his sins, both actions are manifestations of his *exousia* (Matt. 9:6). Aware that the "harvest" was plentiful but the laborers were "few," Jesus extended the power of God given him to his twelve disciples (Matt. 10:1).

His exercise of this power put Jesus in direct opposition to the "power" of the religious leaders. Thus we find the word *exousia* used four more times in one small section (Matt. 21:23–27) after Jesus cleanses the temple. This was discussed on p. 28.

In the ninth use of the word *exousia,* unique to Matthew, *exousia* is shared with the community of his house churches (Matt. 9:8). Following the cure of the paralytic, Jesus showed that "the Son of Man has authority on earth to forgive sins" (Matt. 9:6). Matthew shows Jesus doing the curing, yet the crowds "praised God for giving such authority to human beings" (Matt. 9:8). Shortly thereafter, Matthew's Jesus gives his twelve disciples "authority to expel unclean spirits and to cure sickness and disease of every kind" (Matt. 10:1). According to James Reese,

> The comment of Matthew focuses attention not on the physical cure but on an ongoing expression of the authority of Jesus that was not limited to his earthly existence. It portrays the wonder of the primitive community at sharing in the divine saving power of forgiving sin.

It is true that Matthew does not explicitly state the transfer of authority until the final scene of his Gospel. Yet the organization and dynamism of his presentation tells readers that this transfer is uppermost in the intention of Matthew.[8]

In a post-resurrection narrative, Jesus promises to be with his disciples and in the world through them, and all who are baptized share in the authoritative presence of God by the same power of *exousia* (Matt. 28:16, 18). With this *exousia* the followers of Jesus for all days, throughout the world, will be empowered to continue his presence in the world in the way they teach with authority, forgive others their sins, challenge the abuses of authority by "the authorities," and, above all, be recognized as the ones who "cure sickness and disease of every kind" — be it personal, communal, collective, or environmental.

God is with us in power! This is the reign that must always remain as our "bottom line." It is the reign that must invite to conversion every reign, at every level of the world, which fails to reflect what we now believe to be the Trinitarian reality of the Godhead.

If the Trinitarian reign of God's power is manifest in *exousia,* then the Gospel of the "kingdom of God" proclaimed by Jesus challenged the forces of empire and religion intent on preserving and expanding their own forms of power — worldly powers that undermined the inbreaking of that new order of power in the world. In the eyes of Matthew's Jesus, the power wielded by these forces of control could be found in various forms of imperial and ecclesiastical control (see Matt. 20:25; 10:16–18). The temptation of every disciple, then and now, is to be seduced by or succumb to the kind of abusive authority found in the reigns claiming imperial and infallible power around them, rather than to come under God's kingdom or power.

Today, other words for God's *reign* are God's reality, actuality, presence, dynamic, being, force, strength, existence, subsistence, truth, life, energy, and power. Entering that reign demands that we come under its power, live in this power and proclaim this power as the ultimate reign that rules the universe. Everything in this universe must reflect its maker in ways that reveal the conviction that the Trinitarian reign or reality is at the heart of all other relationships of power because, for the believer, the power of God ultimately legitimates all these forms of power.

Paul's Letters: Grace as God's Empowering Energy at Work in the World

The image of power found in Paul's Letters is in my view more compelling than those in Mark and Matthew, especially when we consider power to be the energy that constitutes all relationships in the universe. Mark and Matthew limited their words for power to *dúnamis* and *exousia*. Paul developed another notion of power that seems to speak more closely to the reality of power that we know from physics as well as faith, phenomenology as well as religion, science as well as spirituality. Paul, like Mark and Matthew, uses the Greek words *dúnamis* (thirty-six times) and *exousia* (seventeen times). But he also used *cháris*, an entirely different word with a meaning that more fully corresponds to the notion of power as it is used in scientific contexts today. *Cháris* constituted the very Gospel Paul proclaimed. Simply stated, *cháris* is God's empowerment of the believer. Its authenticity in the believer is manifest in a life lived under the power or grace of God. It represents the heart of the Gospel of God's reign or power proclaimed by Jesus, as well as the Gospel of Jesus' death and the power that death released in the resurrection.

Paul's "Gospel," built on the subversive notion of the "Gospel" of God's reign originally proclaimed by Jesus, set the believer of his day (and every day) against "the Gospel" of any power system that stands opposed to the power of God at work in the world. Thus Paul would write to the church at Rome, the heart of imperial power, "I am not ashamed of the Gospel; it is the power of God for salvation to everyone who has faith, to the Jew first and also to the Greek. For in it the righteousness of God is revealed through faith for faith; as it is written, 'The one who is righteous will live by faith' " (Rom. 1:16–17).

In her insightful *Paul and the Discourse of Power,* Sandra Hack Polaski makes a strong case for *cháris* to be "shorthand for Paul's entire theological project" and, as such, to be "closely related to notions of power."[9] Indeed, Paul seems to use the words "grace" and "power" interchangeably, as in: "My grace [*cháris*] is sufficient for you, for power [*dúnamis*] is made perfect in weakness" (2 Cor. 12:9; see 1 Cor. 15:8–12).

On the one hand, the power found in Paul's letter refers to God's cosmic energy at all levels of the world (Rom. 12:3), which has been made accessible to all who believe (Rom. 5:1–2; 12:3–8); this grace or power constitutes in the believer the power of God revealed in the death and resurrection of Jesus Christ. As Polaski writes, "God's act of grace makes a new age, a new domain under which the believer now lives."[10] This involves a new way of relating among the believers; a new way of experiencing and expressing power. It is not something that can be gained by one's own power; it cannot be controlled. It is given by God as a pure gift, divine grace, pure empowerment.

Oftentimes the new cosmic power at work in the believers is structurally undermined by other "powers and principalities" (Rom. 8:38; Eph. 3:10; 6:12; Col. 1:16; 2:15) and "elemental powers," which he called *stoichea* (Gal. 4:3, 9; Col. 2:8, 20). This cosmic power has been encapsulated in the Christ in whom all the baptized are graced or empowered to be his presence in the world. The grace or power of God that was revealed in Jesus Christ must now govern the lives of those who believe. The power of the God of the universe must constitute their relationships at every level if they are to be "in Christ" and, ultimately, in God; otherwise they will be living in sin, in alienation from God's power.

We have seen that power has a negative as well as positive expression. Sally Purvis, in her study of Paul's notion of power, finds two "faces" of power: negatively it is manifest as "power as control"; positively, it enlivens individuals, communities, and indeed the whole ecclesial body. As such it becomes "power as life."[11]

This grace or power of God is not handed out unevenly, nor is it hierarchically ordered. As Paul wrote, it was something that he shared with all who believed (Phil. 1:5) in a way that brought them justification or right relationships with God and one another. This meant, according to Polaski, that "the power of God, for which 'grace' is a shorthand expression, is available to all as well; all are included in the 'we' who 'boast in our hope of sharing the glory of God.' The grace of God confers power, and that power belongs rightly to the members of the community."[12]

God's grace (*cháris*) was given to all, but all were given their own unique expressions of that grace in their special charisms (*charismata*). "Grace empowers the community, it makes service to God and to one's neighbor possible, it endows charismata."[13] This grace, if it is authentic, becomes discernible in the lives of the individual members of the community and the community as a whole. The authenticity of the Spirit's power at work in those thus gifted would be manifest in the "fruit of the Spirit," as we will see in the next section.

The Letter to the Galatians
Offering Scriptural Insights for the Power Chart

Paul had preached the Gospel to the people in Galatia without having to explain to these non-Jewish converts anything about "the Law," which he equated with sin and which stood opposed to grace. However, after he left the newly founded church of Galatia, his Gospel — as well as his power — was undermined when outsiders came challenging what he had proclaimed. While much of Paul's resulting Letter to the Galatians deals with the difference in the power of the Gospel versus the power of the proponents of the unnamed "Gospel," it is clear that much of the Gospel itself is Paul's effort to reclaim his power or influence in the Galatian church.

In the letter we find him confronting those whose lives have been influenced negatively by some unnamed opponents. After he had proclaimed the "good news" of God's power and energy to this community, good news that he claimed to be of divine rather than human origin (Gal. 1:11–12), these "reputed ones" used their power to influence the Galatian converts to put themselves under the rule or power of the Law. The Letter to the Galatians is Paul's effort to return the church at Galatia to the authentic power of grace that is expressed in an entirely new way of living. In such a lifestyle "neither circumcision nor uncircumcision is anything; but a new creation is everything" (Gal. 6:15). In other words, a whole new order has been revealed in the Gospel of Jesus Christ; nothing can be the same in their lives, much less their world.

Where he had once convinced them to live according to the grace of the Spirit since they were living in the Spirit (Gal. 5:25), they now had come under the negative dynamics of power and, as such, came to believe they must live according to the dictates of the Law. This, according to Paul, had cut them off from God's power and grace: "You who want to be justified by the Law have cut yourselves off from Christ; you have fallen away from grace.... You were running well; who prevented you from obeying the truth?" (Gal. 5:4, 7).

From here Paul moves into a contrast between a life lived under the Law, which he saw resulting in what he called "the works of the flesh," and a life lived empowered by God, which produced what he called "the fruit of the Spirit." The former deal with dynamics that can be found at the top part of the Power Chart, among which are "enmities, strife, jealousy, anger...and things like these" (Gal. 5:20–21a). Whoever comes under the control of such negative uses of power, he warned, "will not inherit the kingdom of God" (Gal. 5:21c). When the followers of Jesus reveal by their fruits or actions they are living under the power of the Spirit, the church will be alive, as represented on the bottom part of the Power Chart. When they do not, the church will be headed toward corporate destruction; death will result.

Thus Paul writes: "By contrast, the fruit of the Spirit is love, joy, peace, patience, kindness, generosity, faithfulness, gentleness [which we will interpret to be nonviolence], and self-control. There is no law against such things" (Gal. 5:22–23).

With this as our foundation, we now can move to a deeper consideration of the Power Chart. The following chapters take us across the concepts of negative uses of power diagramed at the top of the chart and then address the need to change our way of relating in our use of power. Finally, they carry us across the concepts of positive uses of power diagramed at the bottom of the chart.

Chapter Three

The Positive and Negative Constituents of Power

The Human Condition as the Conflict over Power as Control or Power as Care

Invariably when I give talks on the Power Chart I am asked: "Why do we end up this way? Why do we seem to say we want to care but end up controlling? Is this something inherent to being human?" In response I can only point to what has traditionally been called the contrast between original grace and original sin.

When I was young I never knew that Genesis contains two stories of creation. It was taught as if both accounts were but one story. In catechism classes I learned "there once was a time" when humanity (at least Adam and Eve) lived fully in God's blessing and that God empowered these humans with "preternatural gifts," which included being free from illness and even death. When Adam and Eve came under the power of the serpent, everything changed; this was called "The Fall." When the once-graced couple came under the sway of the serpent (the devil) and committed "original sin," sin entered the world.

Years later, I had to put aside what I learned as a child. Now I learned, under the tutelage of mainstream biblical scholars and the Pontifical Biblical Commission, that the first eleven chapters of Genesis are not truly historical articulations of what happened at one time; they serve as representative efforts of our ancestors in faith to understand what is called "prehistory." Their purpose was not to articulate a doctrine of "original sin" as much as to attempt to understand its *effects* as we experience them in ways that give rise to the great questions of life: Why do we get sick? Why are there floods? Why do we hurt one another? Why do we die? I had to come to understand that although there may never have been, historically, a "Fall," we are indeed fallen.

The "male and female" described in the first account of creation (Gen. 1:26–28), who become the Adam and Eve of the second creation story

(Gen. 2:4–25), are representative of every male and female who will ever live. These stories, in my interpretation, represent the two opposing powers that define every human being. The first power is the original, divinely ordered power of our "I am" that is made in God's image (Gen. 1:26–28). This is opposed, from the beginning of humanity, by whatever stands against God's empowering ways. Our ancestors called this "the serpent." I call the serpent a symbol of all the powers that try to eclipse the power of God at work in us.

As images of God, none of us can say "I am" outside of the *other* "I am" — the "I Am" of God. It is precisely in our relationality that we become a "we" that images the triune Godhead. I cannot say "I am," we have seen, except in relationship. We are made for community, just as God has been revealed as a fully empowered community.

All human relationships must reflect the divine relationality. Because we are made by God in the divine, relational, triune image, we are called by God to that which is good. Consequently, I cannot subscribe to a God who has made us oriented to sin; sin must have its causation outside the reality, the reign, the power, of God. Sin is outside God's reality. Furthermore, I cannot believe in a God who has ordained that humanity be violent, for God would have thus ordered us to be opposed to God's nature. And finally, I cannot accept a God who created "unequal relationality" so that any one human or group of humans is subordinate to another (women to men, for example).

The first account of creation was written in the context of Israel's Exile. Uprooted from the land, without the temple, Israel's world seemed to have ended. They had become accustomed to identify God's presence among them in terms of the land and the temple; now they were without either. The question arose: Where is God? The situation also found them asking a deeper question about themselves: Who are we? This sense of despair and total alienation was captured in the words of Psalm 137: "How can we sing a song to the Lord in a foreign land?"

In the midst of this consternation, the writer(s) of Genesis 1:1–2:4 described a God who did not make this kind of world. They described a God who made order out of the chaos. The Israelites knew that what the story said of "the beginning" and its chaos was symbolic of their chaos and, indeed, of any similar situation that would ever happen in the world. Instead of that darkness, God wanted light.

The story described the chaos of Israel's exile as "*tohu* [empty] *va* [and] *bohu* [without order/form]." Into this chaos God did not just make "light," as we have learned to translate the Hebrew word; God wanted enlightenment, a new, Godly order. In "the darkness" God continually intervenes to enlighten us.

Creation itself shows a certain harmony, even within the chaos, that reveals a kind of interdependence, solidarity, and mutuality. It has been the "sin" of humans that has disrupted creation and that is daily undermining the interdependence, solidarity, and mutuality that creation continually invites us to emulate. For example, a politics of "manifest destiny," an economics of "individualism," and a religion of patriarchy constitute structural sin masquerading as grace. Defining such politics, economics, and religion as God-given and God-ordained conceals the ideological justification for broken relationships in areas God has or-dained to be collaborative. When God is invoked as "willing" such brokenness, the God invoked is idolatrous.

The human condition is that we are born into this world alienated from God, but are continually invited and called by God to become the "I am" that truly images God's care, freedom, and trust; God's healing and healthy ways of building up relationships; the collaboration of the Godhead among its members; God's nonviolence, love, peace, and com-passion for all who are still under the control of the "sin of the world" in all its various expressions. In our effort to define our "I am" in ways that are outside God's "I Am," we sin. The result is the same: broken relationships and power abuses.

We don't need an Adam and Eve to blame for our condition. The human tendency to misuse the power God has given us finds us con-sistently working at cross-purposes with God. God has made us "very good," but some other power or force in us tells us that "very good" is not "good enough." The voice of the serpent, to use the symbol from Genesis, gets the better of us.

Conversion from the serpents in, among, and around us, combined with the embrace of God's life in us in baptism, commit us as disciples of Jesus. In this way we "become like little children." We give up control and allow God's reign to transform our lives. Spirituality is the day-to-day process of moving away from the dynamics at the top part of the Power Chart into our gradual transformation into the dynamics of discipleship that characterize a life defined by the "fruit of the Spirit" found at the bottom part of the chart. In the process we move from "the works of the flesh" to become more influenced and empowered to act by the energy and power of the Spirit, showing forth the Spirit's fruits.

Energizing and Empowering Power

Power is never neutral. As we learn from the great creation stories, power will be expressed either as a force for good or a force for harm. When power is a force for good, it empowers and energizes; it reveals our participation in God's creative power or reign. When people in a community live in positive power relationships they grow in care, as did the members of the early church when they were, like the members of the Trinity, "one heart and soul." "No one claimed private ownership of any possessions, but everything they owned was held in common" (Acts 4:32). In relationships, when we believe we are being treated with equity, fairly and kindly, we grow.

Positive power is expressed in two main ways: affirmation and correction. *Affirmation* is a basic need, if not the core basic need, of every human being. We all need to be held in esteem. We need to feel respected and honored. We need to feel valued and worthwhile. We need significant others in our world to tell us we count. Otherwise, as Linda Loman plaintively appealed to her son Biff in Arthur Miller's *Death of a Salesman,* left to ourselves we are ships by ourselves. We will not only be by ourselves; we will gradually sink. Consequently she appealed to Biff, regarding his father: "Attention must be paid."

"Attending" is a key way to show affirmation. We pay heed; we listen to the thoughts, the feelings and the concerns of the other. When we "at-tend" (from *tendere,* or to hold), we hold the other in safety and security, creating an environment of affirmation and correction, respect and challenge. For many of us who were and are loved in this way, unconditionally or without control, this care becomes the energy that keeps us going in difficult times.

A core concern of parents is their role in affirming their children and creating a nurturing environment. Patterns of parental affirmation and correction must be replicated in the school. As any teacher will attest, most of life in a classroom is spent affirming the students in ways that will challenge them to grow. This dynamic is critical in our culture, given that, as a man who attended one of my workshops told me, by the time we are seventeen years old we have been told fifty thousand times: "You can't." At the same time we've been told five to seven thousand times "Yes, you can."

Too often, the act of correcting or challenging is based in a need to control. Correcting or challenging others will be effective only in an empathetic environment. Without empathy, challenge will be counterproductive. Care is the minimum requirement of every relationship of significance. Correction without care will be perceived as negative.

De-Energizing and Overpowering Power

As the story of Genesis shows, negative expressions of power are universally found in the presence of serpentine forms of exploitation and coercion, manipulation and domination. Such misuses of power represent the "sin of the world" that can be taken away when we come under the reign of God and live empowered lives in the Spirit of God's energy.

I used to think that we in the "developed world" were exempt from exploitative power. I thought of exploitation as the negative influences of forces beyond our ability to remedy, and I would point to political expressions of these in totalitarian states — Cuba under Fidel Castro or the People's Republic of China under the Communist Party. I soon realized, however, that exploitation may not have a clear political expression in a country like the United States, which I call home, but it certainly has an economic face.

For example, workers in this country have learned, via "outsourcing" and "downsizing" that take place even as chief executive pay increases and worker take-home pay decreases,[1] that they may not feel they are under the exact control of others, but they do feel these others don't really *care*. This phenomenon reveals another insight about power: since power is never neutral, the experience of being under the control of forces beyond one's own ability to influence is experienced as the lack of care.

Manipulation is a systematized form of political and economic power. Manipulation that turns wants into needs is the stuff of the market economy. Any parent can tell you about children developing sudden needs in the supermarket because of an attractive, manipulative product display. Advertising transforms our species from *homo sapiens* to *homo consumens*.

When I entered the Capuchin Franciscan brotherhood, the organization was defined by hierarchical dynamics and strict rules and regulations that determined how we would do everything from dressing to dining to getting a tube of toothpaste. It had become an entrenched way of life. Still, when the time came that we were given $25 a month to be spent at our own discretion, a classmate remarked: "Let's go to the mall; I want to see what I need."

When we can be told what we "need" to be accepted and affirmed, and when we can be manipulated to make those "needs" products that may actually harm us (e.g., most forms of fast-food and even some pharmaceuticals), we have become manipulated by outside forces.

Manipulation is essentially dishonest. When it is unconscious, it is understandable as part of the "voices of control" that have tempted humanity from the beginning; when it is conscious, it becomes unconscionable.

Domination is a third manifestation of negative power. Indeed, as she sees relationships, Riane Eisler believes all interaction will be either dominative or participative. Consequently domination is not limited to the superior who tells "inferiors" they can go elsewhere if they disagree; it also happens every Thanksgiving when parents tell their adult children: "I don't care what you think or even what you do when you aren't here. But if you bring him (or her) home, it'll be done this way."[2]

While such a stance between a parent and an adult child indicates the former's way of control, it did not happen overnight. As we will see with care and nonviolence, which need to be continually nurtured, one's upbringing also can nurture dynamics of control and violence. Indeed, Richard Rhodes (himself a victim of childhood abuse) writes that "families are the primary incubators of violence today, as they have always been." He insists that specific forms of violence, such as those perpetrated by criminals, emerge "from social experience, most commonly brutal social experience visited upon vulnerable children. Ignoring it and tolerating the brutalization of children is equally violent, and we reap what we sow."[3]

A fourth negative form of power is coercive power. As with dominative and exploitative power, people are manipulated to come under the control of others through fear and intimidation. The goal of coercive power is compliance. Compliance is often given other names that make it seem less overpowering, names like "obedience" and "submitting to authority." Whatever name it takes, compliance is always the goal of coercion. The means to achieve this goal include threats, cajolery, bullying, or other kinds of negative force to cause fear in those we seek to control.[4]

The need to control is at the heart of all abusive, hurtful, and injurious relationships, whether they take expression in strained family systems, problems with staffing, control of markets, the ability to dictate favorable outcomes in international trade agreements, the direction a political party may take, or who will have ultimate power in structures like that of the male, celibate clergy in the Roman Catholic Church. Groups originally founded for positive purposes can choke off their life-source, their energy, when the need to control dominates the underlying dynamics within the organization.

How do we respond to the negative use of power? There is often little that one can do to challenge it. While some people may have recourse to legal redress, most must develop a "grin and bear it" attitude. Unfortunately they will not be considered "loyal" to the institution. Why? They feel the organization is only "using" them. This makes them less than human in the eyes of those in control.

But what happens when our day-to-day relationships, those between significant others and those among comparative equals, are defined by dynamics of control?

While those exercising the control may be able to get what they want, what happens to the persons negatively affected is one form or another of "getting their backs up." Since the power is a force directed at them, to survive they will have to develop defensive tactics to keep from being violated. They may even "put on a happy face," but inwardly they rebel and become increasingly angry.

The Nonneutrality of Power

Physics tells us that power is never static. It will always either overpower or empower that with which it connects. Consequently, power can never be neutral. It will be a force in relationships that will be either a positive or negative force.

When there's exploitation, manipulation, or domination, or — since relationships can never be neutral — where there is an absence of the right mix of affirmation and correction, that relationship also will be defined by some person's or some group's need to control. I learned this at a weekend workshop I gave to a group of men in Chicago some years ago.

After the Friday night opening session, where I laid out the basic ways we can direct our power — as a force for good through care or a negative force through control — one of the participants began the Saturday morning session by asking: "Last night you said that there is no neutrality in relations of significance. Either they will be a positive or negative force. You said all positive manifestations of power are expressions of care, and that this care is grounded in affirmation and positive reinforcement of others from which there can then (and only then) come correction or challenges. Right?" When I agreed, he continued: "You also said that the negative dynamics of power involve ways of relating that express manipulation and domination, exploitation and coercion, right?" And I agreed again. "However, if it's true that there is no neutrality in relations of significance, wouldn't it also be right to say that we get de-energized and feel overwhelmed when we experience the lack of those core ingredients of care?"

The man was 100 percent right, but I had never thought about that connection. Physics itself confirms the truth of the man's insight. Since everything is connected, the lack of something is experienced as negative energy. The absence of the good equivalently is experienced as the negative. "You don't bring me flowers" and "You don't sing me love songs" say more about the negative dynamics that are occurring in the relationship than any simple forgetfulness. There is no neutrality in a relationship of significance. The conclusion I learned from this member of the group became clear: We must express ourselves in care or the relationship will be experienced by the other not only as a lack of care but as a form of control. The absence is experienced as the negative. It is the lack of the positive that gets experienced as the negative in our relationships. Consequently, as the song goes, the fact that "you don't bring me flowers anymore" and "you don't sing me love songs" can be as hurtful and destructive in a relationship as other forms of neglect.

To give another example, I once read about a woman who complained that her husband of many decades had never once called her by her name. She felt abused and neglected by that very fact. Instead of respecting her by acknowledging her uniqueness and value as signified by her name, he would just say "hey you" when he wanted to attract her attention. She felt deeply hurt by his diminishment of her.

At a global level, especially in the last decade people in the United States have begun to realize the negative consequences and, indeed, the destructive dynamics that can take place when others in the international community begin to see us as a people who don't care what they think, how they feel, and how they would like to be treated. Many would say it's precisely because we have become so self-centered and myopic as a people, combined with the fact of our overwhelming military might and consumeristic lifestyle, that they now rejoice when we are challenged, when we have to "back down," or when we have to admit that we were more preoccupied with our own issues than working together to make the world better.

In my work with groups over the past twenty years, I have increasingly sensed a deeply felt desire of people to want to change the way they use their power, to get to the bottom of what causes negative interactions and behaviors. Together we have unpacked the greatest obstacle to transforming ourselves into positive, empowering and caring human beings: the need to control. We will now take a close look at that need that is pervasive.

Chapter Four

The Dynamics of Control

I am increasingly convinced that, in any human relationship at any level, the need to control is the source of all negativity in our world. Physicists call this negative energy. Psychologists and addiction counselors call it "dysfunctionality." We have seen that in the Judeo-Christian tradition, such negative use of power manifestations reveal "original sin" or "the sin of the world." Though the story of Adam and Eve has now been recognized as a myth, the dynamics it reveals tell the story of every man and woman who has ever lived. Those trying to walk on a spiritual path know that the tasks of getting free of the need to control and moving from this "sin" or "the works of the flesh" into "grace" or "the fruit of the Spirit" are formidable.

Control that is masked as "caregiving" is perhaps one of the most difficult forms. This dynamic is quite evident in a letter to the "Dear Amy" advice column in the *Los Angeles Times*. "Gift-Getting-Gus" wrote:

Dear Amy:

For nearly two years I've been the primary caretaker for my mother. In those two years, my siblings and I have had every kind of disagreement possible. I attribute those to their guilt over not being the caretaker. Some awful things were said.

At one point, I told them that I was not looking for their approval. I also made it clear that I did not want gifts from them. Mind you, I can understand why anyone would want to show gratitude to someone who stepped up when no one else would. Still, I did not want gifts.

Now, several months later, my brother and sister-in-law sent me a gift certificate. Then my sister sent me a gift certificate too.

On one hand, I would love to rise above all the pettiness, be gracious and say, "Thank you." On the other hand, they are blatantly disrespecting the boundaries that I set.

To this Amy responded:

Dear Gus:

Your refusal to accept gifts seems like a play to control your siblings through guilt. As long as you refuse their thanks, you can continue to blame them for being unhelpful and ungrateful. You don't need to use these gift certificates. You can turn them over to your mother or another interested party. You can twist the knife by informing your siblings that you have done so. Or you can let this gesture stand for what it is — an effort to acknowledge you. You can help to heal this family rift by recognizing it.[1]

The need to control arises from self-centeredness or selfishness. We, our group, our nation, our religion, become the center of the universe. When we communicate with others from such a narcissistic stance, the relationship is one-sided, even though we may think we are truly having a dialogue.

When dynamics of control define relationships in a marriage, abuse will not be far behind. When parents rely on control, something is not right in their parenting.[2] When control dynamics enter the workplace, tension will result. When the need to "control markets" defines economic ordering, people and the planet will both be exploited. When a nation needs to control access to the resources that characterize its lifestyle, its people will easily be manipulated to justify war in order to ensure access to those resources. When the obsession to preserve the male, celibate model of "church" defines the dynamics in Roman Catholicism, parishes can be closed with the result that natural groupings of people will be overthrown to protect the church's patriarchal, clerical power structure.

Effectual control is grounded in four forms: manipulation and exploitation, coercion and domination. But it is maintained primarily through fear and intimidation. As I have shared the Power Chart with people around the world, I discover that, no matter what the culture or the religion (but especially Catholicism and Islam), fear and intimidation are the two main methods of exercising control.

In workshops, I often begin my reflections on the dynamics of control by randomly pointing to a person in the audience and asking: "Without going into any detail, could you tell me if you are in or have ever been in a relationship where you have feared or been intimidated by another person or group?" The answer always is "yes." Having established the fact that fear or intimidation has defined that relationship, I then ask: "Would you say that this relationship has been defined by somebody's need to control?" I have never had anyone say "no."

The Role of Fear

Before addressing the negative outcomes of fear, I want to be clear that not all fear is negative. Indeed, fear has positive faces: the adrenaline that energizes us in a race, the call to fight or flight in the face of a threat, the motivation for studying hard for a test or an interview. In the scriptures, fear can be holy or hurtful depending on the kind of power that is involved. Even the phrase "Be not afraid," which is used hundreds of times in the Bible, can refer to one's reaction to a positive or negative manifestation of power, often a divine epiphany. However, the majority of our fears deal with some kind of threat to our security. These are far from holy or helpful.

Negatively, fear can construct in us and among us a prison more over-whelming than iron bars, as in the cartoon showing a man standing in jail clutching the two iron bars in front of him. In the next picture it becomes clear that there are only two bars. The man could be free if he went to the left or the right; instead he is fixated on what he sees immediately in front of him. He lacks hindsight and foresight, and his fear is not grounded in reality. He is paralyzed by fear.

Because fear is primal and might even be seen as part of our genetic wiring,[3] engendering fear in others is an easy way to control them. The specific fear can come in many forms: fear of being rejected, fear of being misunderstood, fear of isolation, fear of failure, fear of being called disloyal or unpatriotic. All fears, I believe, stem from the archetypal fear of being abandoned. When persons close to us threaten to leave, they trigger all the infantile fears connected with separation anxiety. While the words "fear" and "anxiety" have the same Greek origin, *phobos* (from which comes "phobia"), fear and anxiety have the same source: some kind of threat to our security. They differ insofar as fear is the agitation that comes from a threat that is real and immediate, while anxiety involves something that *may be* real but distant; conversely it follows that this same anxiety involves something that *may not be* real and imminent.

Though we are individuals, we are also defined by our life in community. We find in community, in others, refuge in the face of our fears. Unfortunately, our need for security can easily be manipulated; fears surrounding our insecurity make us even more open to manipulation. Carlos Valles explains this well:

> Fear opens us to manipulation. . . . It is one of the aspects of fear that harms us most, as it erodes our personality and mortgages our free-dom. Fear makes us feel insecure, and in our insecurity we readily

turn to whatever can make us feel safe again. We are impatient with insecurity, we cannot bear being long in a state of uncertainty, and we rush to protection and clarity at whatever cost.... Fear makes us shake, in our minds more than in our bodies, and so we grab at the first prop that may steady our faltering stand. In our weakness we fall as easy prey to any dispenser of certainties. Safety first. And, sadly, independence last.[4]

The Manipulability of Our Fears

One of the greatest fears, one that can be easily manipulated, centers on our personal and group fear of the "other," the one who is different. While some adjectives related to power may bring a sense of pride and belonging to those who can identify with them, they also engender fear in those who feel intimidated by their potential to control. Thus we have different responses, depending on where we stand and how we are grouped, to such phrases as "black power," "gay pride," "military might," "Aryan power," "feminist power," "episcopal power," or "the power of globalization."

Having studied how nations go to war following a set of thought pattern,[5] I have watched in sadness the way our leaders have played loose with the facts, but strong on our fears and need for greater security, since September 11, 2001. These led us into a war that seems likely to go on for a long, long time. I find parallels in the Roman Catholic Church: few people, especially those who work within it, are willing to speak against the abuses of power regularly evidenced at its various levels, from the parish priest to the chancery official to the bishop and on up. In my own life every time my conscience challenges me to publicly critique some member of the hierarchy, including the pope, I do so with "fear and trembling."

It is clear that voters' fears are manipulated during election campaigns, especially those at the national level.[6] Once elected, officials continue to play on the fears of citizens, such as they did in the run-up to the Second Iraq War. The connection between the manipulation of citizens' fears and preserving presidential power (i.e., hegemony or control) was well articulated by *New York Times* columnist Bob Herbert at the height of the Second Iraq War. He wrote: "The public's fear is this president's most potent political asset. Perhaps his only asset." He continued: "Mr. Bush wants ordinary Americans to remain in a perpetual state of fear — so terrified, in fact, that they will not object to the steady erosion of their rights and liberties, and will not notice the many ways in which their fear is being manipulated to feed an unconscionable expansion of presidential power."

Linking the abuse of presidential power with another "ism," Herbert declares that such manipulation of fear "is a road map to totalitarianism." Herbert explains:

> Hallmarks of totalitarian regimes have always included an excessive reliance on secrecy, the deliberate stoking of fear in the general population, a preference for military rather than diplomatic solutions in foreign policy, the promotion of blind patriotism, the denial of human rights, the curtailment of the rule of law, hostility to a free press and the systematic invasion of the privacy of ordinary people.[7]

The United States is the strongest nation on the face of the earth, yet its citizens are among the world's most fearful. Robert Frost said, "There is nothing I'm afraid of like scared people."[8] When people's fears are manipulated they will do whatever they are told they need to do to be "safe" and "secure." They will, for example, abdicate universally held norms established among nations regarding torture and support preemptive military strikes as long as it makes them feel safer. But then, when the "enemy" turns out not to be nations but terrorists, they still are willing to attack nations if it means they might feel more secure.

This not only happens to the "masses." It can happen to the very people whose profession is to be a "fifth column" dedicated to seek out and report the truth: the press. Indeed, a key factor among reporters in questioning the build-up that led to the 2003 U.S.-led invasion of Iraq was the fear of being called "unpatriotic." This fear led them to undermine their very "I am" as independent journalists. On the one hand, as columnist Robert Sheer noted, the "media was sucker-punched entirely" by the George W. Bush administration. On the other hand, "There is no doubt that there is an atmosphere of fear in the media of being out of sync with the punitive government." The way this twofold process occurred, Sheer concludes, "has been the most shameful moment for American democracy."[9]

Marketers survive by manipulating our fears. They pit children against parents every time they go to the supermarket — if those children have been watching the commercials during Saturday morning cartoons. Children "come under the influence" of advertisers and their powerful resources. The average parent has no awareness that this unseen force has overwhelmed him or her. But it rears its head throughout the shopping experience and reaches its apogee at the checkout counter: "Mommy, Daddy, buy me that."

Some years ago I said as much in a speech to the Michigan convention of the American Marketing Association. The marketers' retort — "We do not manipulate; we *inform*" — did not hold true for me, and I told them why. Many years ago I went grocery shopping with my brother Pat and his four-year-old son, Craig. When we got to the cereal section, guess what kind of cereals were on the shelves at Craig's line of vision? Captain Crunch, Coco Crisps, and Lucky Charms. And where are the granola and other non-sugared brands? At Pat's eye-level. Of course, Craig already knows what's good for him; he's already been "informed" by the marketers. But Pat doesn't know that, so he says: "Craig, that's not good for you." Then Craig begins to cry and Pat gets angry. At Craig! He thinks Craig is trying to manipulate him; however, not only has Craig already been manipulated by the marketers; his trust in his father has been eroded. When the marketers heard this story, they became sensitized as Moms and Dads who experience the consequences of their success at work in the frustration of their shopping at the supermarket. I can only hope they have continued to think that way as they do their work.

Maybe we have become more sophisticated now, and so we are not surprised when the *Wall Street Journal* carries a cautionary column warning investors: "Don't Get Hit by the Pitch: How Advisers Manipulate You."[10] We see more clearly how others — be they individuals in our families, advertisers on our televisions, money advisers or politicians visiting us at election time — manipulate our fear. Yet we find it hard to admit that we often do the same thing. One of the most powerful ways we reinforce the dynamics of control that may characterize our lives is to deny its influence on our relationships. When I was writing this book, I happened to be giving a retreat to a group of women religious. After a talk on nonviolence, in which I showed that all violence stems from an individual's, a group's, or an institution's need to control, a ninety-two-year-old woman sought me out. "I never thought I was a controlling person," she said, "until I read a book a couple of years ago. It asked a bunch of questions and then gave me a way of rating how controlling I was. I was surprised at the degree I still was defined by my need to control. That made me realize I had to change. I'm a different person now."[11] She learned the wisdom of acting on the real challenge facing her — and all of us: to change her framework of thinking from fear which justifies controlling others to a new way of care engendering hope.

The Role of Intimidation

Intimidation differs from fear insofar as fear plays on our emotions; intimidation more directly challenges our well-being itself. Intimidators have various methods at their disposal:

- They threaten to use power or control to get others to do what they want them to do.
- They use coercion or force to get what they want from others.
- They convince others that they (the intimidators) are more powerful or forceful than they really are.[12]

Intimidators dominate through coercion and other controlling tactics that can be verbal or nonverbal. They act in such a way that none dare correct or challenge. Some intimidators make effective terrorists; their method involves indiscriminate threats that paralyze opponents. Their goal seems to be the need to get what they want in whatever way is needed, no matter who may be used to do so.

Few people, I believe, consciously want to intimidate; in fact, I know from my own experience that I can honestly say I never wanted to intimidate others. But I did. How? It was not my physical size, stature, or strength that created fear in others. Invariably it revolved and still revolves around my personality. Because I am more of an extrovert, I could overpower those who are more introverted. Because I am a quick thinker, I could overwhelm those who need more time to process information — "You never can get a word in with Mike Crosby." I also have a good store of knowledge in the fields of my expertise; others without such information would feel helpless in a conversation. Because I can be idealistic and persistent, others have felt de-energized by my intensity.

It took me a long time to realize that how I was using my power in the form of control (thinking my ways were the only ways) was engendering fear in others; I intimidated them. I had to decide if I would continue using my power in this way or if I would change my way of trying to influence others. Upon reflection, I have come to admit that I always knew I was a person who liked to be "in control." However, I did not think that I maintained control through fear and intimidation. I understood fear and intimidation as the vehicles through which dominating persons were able to get their way; I recognized intimidating behavior in others, and, for sure, I observed it in the dynamics of the Roman Catholic Church at its institutional level. When I finally realized that my behavior sometimes intimidated others, it also became clear that I had become a mirror image of the very thing I was so adamantly against.

Another way I tried to maintain control was by selective interpretation of the facts or the components of an issue or situation. In my obsession to be "right," I would not attend to other ways of looking at a problem, at different perspectives that might be considered and alternative ways of approaching a situation. In other words, in my desire to be right, I *had to be right*. The flip side of this coin of "righteousness" is that I *could not admit to being wrong*. In the process I became an ideologue. As a result I tried to control what people knew so that they would think my way and, above all, do what I thought was necessary for the outcome I desired. Having seen how I manipulated the truth to fit "my truth," I now can sense more clearly ideology (on the left or the right) when it is being used. While I now might not be afraid of ideologues or intimidated by them, I can understand how others can easily be overwhelmed by abuse of power in the service of an ideology.

The Role of "Control Freaks"

In her study of the nature of violence, Whitney Bauman showed the inevitability of violence when power gets more and more concentrated in groups within societies. She concluded, following insights of Hannah Arendt:

> The more monolithic the ethos and government of a society become, the more violent that society becomes. Almost paradoxically, history shows that in times of political uncertainty, often times a result of political diversity and change — the very ingredients of thinking together — ideologies, usually monolithic in nature, begin to grab hold of the minds of many, especially those in power. If those in power begin to fear that their power is threatened or losing ground, the reaction is often first to substitute real thinking with ideologies in order to maintain power. These ideologies erode space and thus set the conditions out of which violent actions *can* occur. In this case, power gives way to violence in the face of fear, perhaps first as fear of losing power.[13]

What happens, though, when an ideology is genuinely perceived by the follower of it (whether an individual or a group) to be "the truth"? On the individual level it can result in aggrandizement of the self and belittling one's opponent. At the group level it can mean the breakup of families over different interpretations of monies left by a deceased member. At the level of nations it can mean invasions and preemptive military strikes. Within a religion, like Roman Catholicism, it invites groupings into those deemed to be true believers and those who are heretical. Among religions it can be holy wars. All such forms of violence are ideologically reinforced and justified. The more monolithic the power involved, the more violence will be justified, even in the name of God.

Control over others not only takes place through fear and intimidation. As our Power Chart makes clear, the very antithesis of control occurs when freedom and trust define a relationship rather than fear and intimidation. Thus it should be no surprise that "control freaks" fear others' freedom as well. They therefore do not seem to have great qualms when they undermine that freedom, or take away the ability of others to define their unique "I am." Consequently, they also find it very difficult to trust anyone and, as a result, to entrust themselves to anyone. Genuine care is jeopardized when control defines the relationship.

When genuine care defines a relationship, it is grounded in the kind of respect given others because of their basic dignity as persons. It follows then that when control defines a relationship, committing an indignity of one kind or another will characterize the way of relating by the person in control. Speaking at the United Nations, Dr. Joerg Bose defined dignity as "something to do with social relationships, having to do with worth or honor, something conferred by others." At the same time, indignity is "something caused by experiencing trauma and victimization conveyed to victims through experiencing utter powerlessness and worthlessness."[14]

What makes control freaks tick? According to the psychotherapist, author, and trainer Philip Chard, "Their malady pivots on the issue of trust." He explains: "They simply don't trust people around them, whether at work or home. Their insistence on being 'in charge' of their world and everyone in it demonstrates how little confidence they have in others." As he explains further their way of exercising power, Chard holds out little hope that they will change: "By nature, control freaks usually lack behavior flexibility and are reticent to change, particularly in response to feedback."[15] On the part of those who live and work with such people, the consequence will be a feeling of being abused.

Let us now take a closer look at what we mean by abuse in its broader aspects as an outcome of the need to control.

Chapter Five

Why More of Us Are Abusers Than We'd Like to Admit

I concluded the previous chapter by noting that control over others takes place through (1) fear and intimidation and (2) the denial of the freedom of the other. As a consequence, those affected by negative power experience themselves as victimized. They see the other's use of power as abusive. This brings me to the second definition that has deeply influenced the thoughts I am sharing in this book. The clearest definition of "abuse" comes perhaps surprisingly from a religious group that has been identified with abuse of power possibly more than any other entity in the United States: the Roman Catholic bishops. According to one of their 1992 documents (in which they speak of "domestic abuse" and not "ecclesiastical abuse"), abuse is "any way one controls another through fear and intimidation."[1] Abuse can occur one-on-one; it can occur when individuals dominate groups and when small groups of individuals control institutions. Such organizations can range from political groups to corporations and from religious institutions to nations themselves. Other words for abuse are hurt, pain, and injury. Where such dynamics occur at any level of life we find sickness, ill health, and pathology.

According to Sigmund Freud, the founder of modern psychotherapy, "It is impossible to escape the impression that people commonly use false standards of measurement — that they seek power, success and wealth for themselves and admire them in others, and that they underestimate what is of true value in life."[2] While recognizing these negative forces creating pathology in individuals, Freud also pointed to their debilitating and unhealthy impact on the social body of peoples as a whole. He wrote that the two processes — "that of the cultural development of the group and that of the cultural development of the individual" — are always "interlocked." For this reason, he argued, "some of the manifestations and properties of the super-ego can be more easily detected in its behavior in the cultural community than in the separate individual."[3] While tempted to apply this theory to the "super-ego" of the United States, he

55

decided, as an Austrian, to leave that task to the American people. However, increasingly alarmed at the destructive and abusive behavior that can flow from aberrations connected with a collective "super-ego," he spoke of the need for people in the future "to embark upon a pathology of cultural communities."[4] In other words, Freud recognized the need to treat the illness or pathology in society itself that came from various forms of abuse.

Returning to the way we as individuals can be, by definition, abusers (in ways that apply equally to groups, nations, and even religions) in the way we control, at the individual level, I find that although this control can be exercised in ways that are intentional, people most often function from control dynamics unintentionally or unconsciously. Few of us *want to abuse others.* In fact we would be affronted if someone would call us an "abuser." However, if we would change the word "abuse" to "hurt" or "injure," or even to create "dis-ease," I think we'd have to admit that some of the ways we may have exercised power vis-à-vis others indeed did result in these others being hurt; we did inflict pain. This occurred when these others felt overwhelmed by us because of the strength (i.e., power) of our presence, their inability to feel equal to the power of our personality, their sense of being made powerless by the strength of our intensity or their inability to feel equal to our articulation of ideas.

The Overpowering Quality of Some Personalities

As I have stated elsewhere in this book, I am an intense person. Some would say I'm a "Type A" personality. For those familiar with the ancient Sufi Enneagram, which illustrates variations in personality types, I think I am in one of the groups that are "head" people. I'm also deeply committed to right wrongs, to speak the truth to power, and to try to undo social injustice. However, as I mentioned in the previous chapter, I have examined the way I function and I have learned that I have been an "abuser." Other people have often felt overwhelmed by me; I have discovered that some of them have felt abused by the power of my presence and personality.

As a person who (unconsciously) controlled others because of my personality, I realized I had to change my behavior. Why? If power is "Michael Crosby's ability to influence," the way I was using my power was disrespectful of others' power. If people kept quiet in a conversation because they felt I would not treat them as an equal, or if they were afraid I might "walk over them" when a difference of opinion ensued, or if they did what I wanted not out of genuine agreement with me but because of fear and intimidation, I was, by definition, abusing them.

When we apply these insights to the behavior (personality) of political, economic, and religious forces in the world, we often come to the same conclusion: those who overpower others will be unable to recognize that the very way they are trying to control their members or exploit and manipulate others will be seen as manifestations of dominance. Indeed, the U.S. Catholic bishops, though they have authored a document on domestic violence, have yet to truly apologize for their abuse of power in the pedophilia scandals of the recent decades. Why? They must have convinced themselves that they are not abusers; they are bishops, called by God.

Politically, we find abuse taking place when a U.S. secretary of state invites Europe to join in the "mission" and "call" of the United States to bring (its form of) freedom and democracy to the world and, at the same time, supports preemptive military strikes to ensure our way of life.[5] Economically, we find this in the global impact of the "McDonaldization" and "Wal-Martinizing" of cultures. In a religion like my own, we see ongoing abuse against women and homosexual members inflicted by the male, celibate clerical caste that runs the organization of the Catholic Church. However, when other nations, cultures, women, and homosexuals critique such behavior as "abusive," the abusers will be quick to label their critics as "unpatriotic," "treasonous," "Neanderthal," "communist," "disloyal," and "heretical." This phenomenon brings me to the next section, on the way our words can reflect real abuse.

"The Wounds of Words"

Years ago I read an article called "The Wounds of Words" in *Newsweek*. The article began with the story of a woman who lived in fear of her verbally abusive husband's return from work each day. The woman said: "My self-esteem and the whole world started going down." The article continues:

> When Archie Bunker called Edith a dingbat and admonished her, "Stifle yourself," we laughed. But in real life, verbal abuse is anything but funny. It can warn of physical abuse to come — and even all by itself can destroy a relationship. While most everyone loses his temper now and then, and even says mean things to a loved one, the verbal abuser has a different style and a different motivation. He uses words and emotions (like anger and coldness) to

punish, belittle and control his partner, and he does it compulsively and constantly. He rarely apologizes and shows little empathy [i.e., "care"]. Although men and women have carped at each other since Eden, verbal abuse is suddenly a hot new issue among professions who study and treat domestic violence.[6]

Apart from physical injury, verbal abuse can be more destructive in a relationship than physical abuse because verbal abusers often try to undermine one's self-image and even destroy self-esteem. They find ways to tear apart self-image. Their goal, conscious or not, is to make the other feel powerless. Thus, when we tell others they are "stupid" or "incompetent," we can destroy, or at least undermine, their ego, their sense of self. How many times have I heard one party in marriage counseling say she or he feels totally rejected upon being called a "dumb shit" or a "lazy bastard."

Part of our "I am" is equated with our name. To name another is to have power over that person. That's why some Jews to this day never use God's name when they speak. The name identified with my "I am" also can be violated. Thus to call people names undermines their identity and can render them powerless. I'll never forget the story of the fireman who pulled a child from a burning house. Trying to keep the child conscious, he kept asking: "What is your name?" Finally the child opened his eyes and said, "Stupid." We can only imagine the intensity of verbal abuse that led to this child's response to the fireman.

Verbal abuse need not always be expressed in earthy language. It occurs when I relate to someone who is more introverted who gets overwhelmed by my extroverted behavior. It occurs when I don't give others a chance to talk or share their ideas before I move on. All these represent forms of verbal abuse. Whether I call you a "dumb shit" or dominate you in the conversation, the result for you is the same: you feel hurt; you see yourself as abused. You feel that I really don't care about what you think, how you feel, or what you do.

While many would be able to see the violence involved in being called nasty names or referred to in derogatory terms by others, nonverbal dynamics in a marriage or group also can be abusive and, therefore, destructive of healthy dynamics and connectedness. Oftentimes this is couched by people in words that would make their "silent treatment" sound downright positive for themselves — and for others as well. It gets expressed in the person who says: "I find that whenever so-and-so and I get together, it seems we argue. So I find it better if I just don't talk to him." And then they add, somewhat shamefully: "Do you think this is right?"

I found it very difficult to admit that I was a nonverbal abuser. Others have been afraid to challenge me, and still others feel intimidated by me, so I, by definition, have been abusive in this way too. I may never have wanted to attack another, but others have been anxious in my presence. There may be no physical abuse, but one's self-image may be shattered, one's feelings trampled, and one's accomplishments belittled. Admitting this "exact nature of our wrongs" is not easy to do, any Twelve Stepper will tell us. But I find that it is a transformative exercise to liberate us from unacknowledged negative aspects of ourselves that impair our relationships.

The Overpowering Effect of Some Social Arrangements

If the term "abuser" is applied to ourselves as a nation, we quickly deny the allegation. Yet, in poll after poll, we find people of virtually every other country in the world seeing us as the world's bully, trying to overpower them in trying to make the world conform to our image. At the same time, citizens in this country do not agree that we are seen as the abuser in our foreign policy and economic dominance.[7] While the average U.S. citizen might be in denial about such expressions of U.S. imperialism, American business leaders themselves have come to admit its existence. They have acknowledged that such perceptions of our abusive ways are now undermining their own corporate bottom lines. In other words, the abuse by the United States toward others is beginning to destroy us. Thus, an article in the "Money and Business" section of the *New York Times* noted, "anti-U.S. sentiment isn't just unpleasant. It hurts the bottom line."[8] In other words, it's bad for the health of the economy.

From this perspective it's no wonder that people talk about abuse as a form of violence that affects *public health*. Over 1 million people who have been injured as a result of abuse or violence are seen each year by emergency medical personnel. They are victims of domestic abuse, child abuse, and elder abuse, as well as assaults and handgun-related violence.[9]

Abuse obviously affects public health, and more and more we are realizing that public health itself will get better or worse depending on how social, political, civic, and economic forces build up or debilitate nations. This conviction led to the founding of the Institute for Innovation in Social Policy. One of its tasks was to create a "report card" to measure the nation's well-being, beyond the traditional "state of health" identified with economic factors such as the gross domestic product, consumer confidence, or employment rates. Each year the Institute measures the "State of the Nation" and all fifty states using indicators ranging from child abuse to unemployment and from drunken driving deaths to average weekly wages. (I first heard about this in 2003 while lecturing in New Mexico. The people in the state were not happy to read that it ranked at the bottom for its overall social health.[10]) Similarly, the Worldwatch Institute issues an annual *State of the World* report in which the health of nations is measured by objective indices.[11] One of these deals with the treatment of women.

After ten years in an abusive marriage, Samia Sarwar tried to get a divorce. On April 6, 1999, she was shot dead in her lawyer's office in Lahore, Pakistan. The murder was instigated by her own parents. As with hundreds of other murders of women and girls committed each year in Pakistan in the name of family or community honor, no one was brought to justice for the crime.

Similarly, in 1994 a twenty-seven-year-old Pakistani man pumped seven bullets into his younger sister. His widowed mother and uncles told him to kill the seventeen-year-old after she eloped with her boyfriend, staining the family's honor. He resisted for three months because "I loved my sister and didn't believe she deserved to die." But then the neighbors stopped talking to him, the grocer refused to sell him bread, the local imam said he was disobeying Allah, and his mother threatened to curse the milk she had breast-fed him. "So he gave in."[12]

"Honor killings" violently enforce notions of male prerogative in nations whose laws condone such behavior or whose male-controlled courts dismiss those accused of such behavior. However, they are being increasingly challenged. Indeed, the United Nations has called all forms of violence against women "a manifestation of historically unequal power relations between women and men" and a means by which this inequality will be structurally ensured. As a result, groups like Amnesty International are promoting campaigns to stop domestic violence against women.[13]

I find it paradoxical, as a Roman Catholic clergyman, that the bishops of my own country would also address the issue of domestic violence — not so much because of the need to have this topic addressed from pulpits in our church but because of what was a key motivator for them to write this document.

Their 1992 statement *When I Call for Help: Domestic Violence against Women*[14] was a substitute effort that seemed necessary when a years' long effort to deal with the real issue of "women in the church" failed even though they had listened to women's thoughts on the subject. When they found themselves floundering because they could not honestly address the issue of the constitutionally and canonically mandated inequality between women and men in the church that would be considered religiously sanctioned abuse, they found a way to finesse the issue of power and began final touches on a document. When they submitted their results to the Vatican for its approval, the verdict was returned: not acceptable. A main reason, according to the Vatican, was the "flawed methodology" used by the bishops. In other words, the ones who perceived themselves as possessing "the truth" had nothing to learn from women. Listening to women is a flawed methodology in writing a document on how women are abused by systems of unequal power relations.[15]

Then the U.S. bishops received a proposed document on women from the Vatican. But its contents were such that the bishops themselves rejected it for fear of how its contents would be received. Unwilling to address the fact of the unequal power relationships that resulted in this institutionalized form of abuse (which almost every woman in the employ of parishes and chanceries can relate to), the bishops signed on to a document on *domestic* violence, or violence in the house, rather than violence in the "household of faith."

The Role of Denial and Delusion in Sustaining Abuse

Abuse, especially by people involved in fiduciary relationships (relationships of trust) such as parent and child, counselor and client, minister and parishioner, often goes unreported because the victim has been led to believe that she or he must have caused the abuse. However, when the abuser is confronted, a typical response is denial.

When we examine why addicts remain under the debilitating power of alcohol and drugs, including nicotine, as well as sexual addictions and other relational addictions, denial of the negative force of the addictive agents and processes is one of the main culprits. When we apply the learnings about addictions and the devastation they can wreak on family systems to the dysfunctional systems sustained by abuse like sexism and patriarchy, elitism and clericalism, we find the same thing: denial that the power dynamic exists as abuse. Anne Wilson Schaef derived this discovery of macro-denial in systems from her experience of denial in dealing with addicts. She writes: "Denial allows us to avoid coming to terms with what is really going on inside us.... We cannot be alive in a system based upon denial. It leaves us no real avenue to deal with our reality."[16] It is the major defense mechanism.

Having met quite a few perpetrators of sexual abuse of minors, I have been intrigued by their denial of the fact. Why, for instance, do parents accused of abuse adamantly deny they did anything wrong when all evidence says they did indeed sexually abuse their children? One day it dawned upon me that it's a matter of protecting that which is deepest in their psyche. Since the abuse of an innocent child by a parent undermines the "I am" of that child so severely, as well as the "I am" of the one in power, any self-reflective person would almost automatically deny the possibility that he or she could have violated the fiduciary relationship so severely. Further, I believe they are unwilling to face the facts of their abusive behavior because to do so would be tantamount to publicly declaring that they have failed in a critical role entrusted to them by society: the raising of a child in an environment of safety, free of abuse.

More subtle and even more devastating than denial of abuse is to delude oneself that abuse is "good for" a child — or anyone for that matter. Alice Miller exposed this "poisonous pedagogy" in her classic: *For Your Own Good: Hidden Cruelty in Child-Rearing and the Roots of Violence.*[17] When abuse is sanctioned as necessary or even meritorious, we are not far from religiously sanctioned violence and jihads. Such delusion involves defining a lie as truth, calling injustice a matter of righteousness, and violence as the will of God. Denial represents a form of self-deception, whether that "self" is an individual, group, or members of a group within an institution. It represents the act of standing firm in a belief or conviction that is not true. Delusion is the ultimate protection in self-defense when confronted with our personal, communal, or collective abuse.

As has been noted, other words for abuse are "being injured," "being violated," "being hurt." When such dynamics define a relationship at any level of life in our increasingly connected world, that relationship will be headed toward destruction. Where such destructive patterns are in place and built on controlling forces, the relationship will be gradually destroyed and the anger of the abused will percolate in various forms of resentment and even spill over as rage.

I have given anger a central position on the Power Chart as the potent reactive force in the negative uses of power and will now turn attention to an in-depth discussion of the forms that it takes when it goes in that direction.

Chapter Six

Destructive Dynamics
Fueled by Anger

You will note that on the Power Chart anger is on the same parallel as power. Like power, anger is neutral. It can be a negative as well as a positive force. Indeed, the scriptures seem to acknowledge this: "Be angry but do not sin" (Eph. 4:26). If we look at the Gospel and interpret it the same way as Reverend William Sloan Coffin, we'd even be saying, with him: "Jesus was angry over 50 percent of the time, and it's very dangerous to try to improve on Jesus. The anger needs to be focused, but anger is what maintains your sanity. Anger keeps you from tolerating the intolerable."[1]

Whether one agrees with Sloan Coffin or not, it is clear that anger need not always be considered sinful or negative; it can actually represent an occasion of grace and result in the promotion of good.

Anger is a normal emotion that helps us deal with negative experiences of power or lack of enough positive expressions of power. It involves a reaction to others' efforts to control us through fear and intimidation or their withholding of care from us. Anger can represent a reaction to a threat to our "I am," to our integrity, to our personal autonomy and freedom. As such anger can be a positive force or a negative force in our lives and world; it can be constructive or destructive. To better understand anger's dynamic, it is helpful to look at the causes of anger.

The Causes of Anger

Our word for anger comes from the root *angh*. It refers to one's reaction to a feeling of being constricted and restricted, narrow and tight. Anger arises from a feeling or experience of such dynamics as well as being overwhelmed and pressured. It results from a sense of being threatened in our "I am," or the image of our "I am" that we have cultivated in response to the "serpents" in our lives. The feeling of anger has many forms: frustration, indignation, hostility, as well as other forms we will consider more fully later: rage and resentment.

In addition to threatening our "I am," the causes of anger are twofold. Anger results when (1) we experience control, injustice, or violence, and (2) we experience neglect, the lack of care we need to be healthy individuals.

Anger occurs when we experience others' use of power in negative or abusive ways that adversely affect us or those about whom we are concerned. It comes as a reaction to relationships gone awry, to one's experience of injustice. A classic expression of this kind of anger is found in the reaction of Jesus when he entered the temple in Jerusalem and found its purposes being violated.

When we become conscious of others trying to manipulate or exploit us, to dominate or coerce us so that they can control us, we get angry. Sometimes, if we are more or less equal to them, we might immediately react and challenge the behavior. When this occurs, the relationship, being more-or-less balanced, will reflect dynamics of basic equality. In unbalanced relationships, such as employer/employee or parent/child, the person may have to suppress anger in order to survive. At the same time, however, that person's anger will increase. In other words, anger arises when our basic needs around the triad of power-objects — power itself, our material things, and our image — are disrespected, belittled, or undermined.

Anger can also occur when we experience conflicts that will not be resolved because we or the other is unwilling to go through a conflict resolution process. Or it arises in reaction to direct experiences of violence in the form of some kind of force that inflicts injury to us or those we care about. Anger also happens when people show dislike or hatred toward us. Finally, it comes when we realize that people really "don't care" or are indifferent toward those to whom they should be showing care. This makes us feel like we "make no difference" to the way they relate to us. We are nothing. This generates anger.

In the second case, anger arises when we don't experience the various forms of care that would make us healthy individuals who are respected and loved. Some of the deepest forms of anger result from expressions of neglect: "You never loved me; you always liked _____ more than me."

Anger also arises when we find people "missing the forest for the trees." Jesus felt such anger when he challenged the Pharisees and scribes because they stressed religious externals but overlooked the internals. Or when "for the sake of your tradition," such as care for the temple, they nullified the basic law of care for parents (Matt. 15:6–9).

When we examine some of the principal ways our anger gets expressed, I find two main forms: rage and resentment. Both arise from a sense of being made powerless in a relationship because of some or all the dynamics on the top of our Power Chart, as well as a perceived withholding of the possibility of experiencing the dynamics on the bottom part of the chart.

Anger as Rage

In 2005, Academy Award-winner Russell Crowe pleaded guilty to third-degree assault after a plea bargain. He initially had been charged with assault and criminal possession of a weapon. The weapon was a phone that he threw at a Manhattan hotel concierge when he had trouble calling his wife in Australia from his room. A moment of anger spiraled into rage, then violence.

Rage, as I see it, comes from a feeling of powerlessness in the face of a force greater than us. It arises spontaneously from a sense of being violated. As such it can be immediate and short-lived. Almost all of us experience it now and then. However, if rage becomes chronic it can easily slip into paranoia, a sense of being attacked personally, and result in further forms of violence. It can also come from a sense of one's own importance and privilege.

More of us have experienced road rage in reaction to others' driving. Our society has coined words describing new types of rage besides road rage. Now we have sky rage, checkout counter rage, sideline rage, and school rage to such a degree that *Time* magazine would feature a piece on kindergarten children "acting out in really outrageous ways."[2] As I researched for this book I learned of two other kinds of rage. E-mail rage: my local paper reported that a Milwaukee attorney was awarded "$1.4 million for a scathing series of e-mails sent by a former client."[3] The business section of the *San Francisco Chronicle* featured an article called: "Outsourcing Outrage" with the subtitle: "Indian Call-Center Workers Suffer Abuse."[4]

Meanwhile, the original rage, found on highway after highway, continues unabated. Jerry Sola demonstrates that even road rage can be overcome. He was returning to his Chicago suburb in 1999 when the driver in front of him slammed on his brakes. Sola got so infuriated that he gunned his engine, sped by the driver, and cut in front of him. When they both had to stop for a red light, Sola grabbed a golf club from his backseat. "I was just about to smash his windshield or do him some damage," the former police officer recalls. "Then it hit me: 'What in

God's name am I doing? I'm really a nice helpful guy. What if I killed a man, went to jail, and destroyed two families over a crazy, trivial thing?' I got back in my car and drove away."

Shocked by his experience, Sola has worked conscientiously to rein in his rage. "I am a changed person," he says, "especially behind the wheel. I don't listen to the news on the car radio. Instead, I put on nice, soothing music. I force myself to smile at rude drivers. And if I feel myself getting angry, I ask a simple question: 'Why should I let a person I'm never going to see again control my mood and ruin my whole day?' "[5] It's a simple question, but a wise one to ask yourself when tensions rise.

Anger as Revenge

In my life I have found it immediately rewarding when I have heard about some mishap occurring to someone with whom I have a difference. It's the proverbial delight we experience when our "enemy" slips — even on a banana peel! However, I have also discovered, given its place on the Power Chart as a destructive force that continues unhealthy dynamics, revenge may bring about short-term rewards, but it does so at the expense of long-term health in our own hearts as well as in our way of relating with others.

Revenge, a form of anger-release, is one of the first forms of anger expressed in the Bible and is found throughout the pages of many a novel, and it remains a hot topic. In its January 12, 2007, centerfold, the *National Catholic Reporter* featured the experiences of many of its readers on the subject. Less than two weeks later *Business Week* had a cover feature entitled: "Revenge: The Power of Retribution, Spite, and Loathing in the World of Business." Although it showed how revenge has been at the heart of many corporate intrigues in the last decade, its definition of revenge rings true: "a response to a perceived injustice or what psychologists call narcissistic injury, known to you and me as a wounded ego."[6] Given that definition, it follows that a way of reducing our tendency toward revenge is to reduce our ego needs. If I have fewer ego needs, there will be little to threaten my ego and, therefore, less need for compensation for any bruises my ego might incur.

The disastrous events of 9/11/01 have resulted in a widespread re-action of anger through revenge. One commentator wrote: "Although there was a good deal of grief, sadness and feeling connected to loss and suffering expressed, what was most striking was the level of anger that emerged. The anger was largely contained and couched in the garb of rational intellectual discourse, but the intensity of the rage was palpable."[7]

Anthropologist Stephen Juan has found at least six reasons retaliation seems so central to our psychological makeup: (1) as a defense function to keep from being attacked (again); (2) to get pleasure or some kind of vindication; (3) to restore lost pride; (4) to undo the shame and humiliation from some kind of perceived injury; (5) to protect oneself from grieving over some kind of loss or separation or anxiousness; and (6) to develop or maintain self-esteem.[8]

Despite the fact that the Judeo-Christian scriptures include the often-quoted line, " 'Vengeance is mine,' says the Lord," it seems that many of us have enough desire for revenge that we have appropriated it as a destructive force in our lives and relationships.

Anger as Resentment

While rage normally is a reaction that is immediate and short-lived, and revenge can be both immediate and short-lived as well as ongoing, resentment often results from a sense of some past grievance that simmers over an extended period of time. Resentment is like a stray cat, someone once told me: "If you keep feeding it, it will never leave you." Let me give you a personal experience to illustrate this point.

Some years ago I worked at a social agency. For years, the agency's director performed his job so collaboratively that everyone felt ownership in the agency, its direction, and its programs. When he left the agency another man was hired by our board of directors to be the director. He took a more hierarchical approach to the job, which put him at odds with the three of us "power people" on the staff, myself included. As a result he felt threatened and tried to find ways he could act as though he was "in charge." I told him that I thought his approach was unnecessary and that any of us at the agency could run it ourselves.

After a year of such functioning, it came time for the director's contract to be renewed. For various reasons, including his basic approach, I felt that he was the wrong person for the job, so I wrote to the board. In my letter I told the board exactly what I had said to the director, face-to-face, earlier in the year. When the board met they were not prepared to decide whether or not to renew the contract. They asked for a month to consider the issue I had raised. After the month they decided the director had not been given fair warning, so they renewed his contract for another year.

Now, with the assurance of another year in his position (i.e., power), the director called me in. He told me he was upset I had written the board without sending him a copy of the letter. Although I pointed out that I had said nothing in the letter that I had not told him to his face, he put me on probation.

Never in the history of my group, to my knowledge, had any of us been put on probation. And now a man I considered to be quite incompetent for the task of director itself had taken that action against me. I was angry. And I let the anger simmer into resentment.

I found that my resentment, while aimed at the director, was consuming me. I became preoccupied with finding ways I could work my way around him. I woke up thinking about it; I went to bed thinking about it. It affected my every moment, including my quiet time for reflection and recouping. When I realized that my resentment was destroying me, rather than the director, I knew I had to change and I sought help.

A key element in Twelve Step spirituality addresses the issue of resentments. As long as we hang on to our resentments, they will control us. Resentments have a way of destroying our "I am." Resentment is the opposite of gratitude. It is often expressed in a kind of chronic complaining or negativity. Resentful people see the glass half-empty; as a result their lives become quite empty as well.

Anger as Passive-Aggressiveness

Unlike rage, revenge, or resentment, which are forms of expressed anger, repressed anger is manifest in various forms of passive-aggressiveness. Those who act out anger in a passive-aggressive manner may come off as "nice," yet they find subtle ways to obstruct, procrastinate, forget, or intentionally become inefficient. The psychologist Robert Wicks notes that passive-aggressiveness is a "psychological cancer" that can destroy a relationship; it can create "communal psychopathology."[9] It gets lodged in unspoken thoughts, feelings that are not made clear, and behavior oriented to hurt. Some personalities and some nationalities have cultivated this form of anger quite effectively.

Mary M. O'Shaughnessy notes that passive-aggressive behavior "is the most difficult to confront and to deal with effectively." As she explains it:

Passive-aggressive behavior is characterized by *withholding* ourselves now from persons, places, and events to which we have in the past committed ourselves. People, situations, and social endeavors are left hanging, unattended, and in the lurch with no advance warning of our change of mind, our change of heart. We delay and postpone dealing with important issues, and we put off making decisions which affect our lives as well as the lives of others. We retaliate and punish both ourselves and others in and through the withholding of our time and our energy in a specific endeavor. When we are passive-aggressive we withhold our communication and poor participation from people who have a right to expect our direct sharing and our active involvement in their lives or in a given project or endeavor.[10]

O'Shaughnessy notes something that I never realized about those who are passive-aggressive: many become addicted to drugs, alcohol, food, nicotine, or work. In so doing we "withdraw from legitimate relationships and social interactions and reach out dependently to crutches of one kind or another."[11]

Given my personality and my nationality, I find more than my share of passive-aggressiveness in my ways of relating. For instance, I know that when I act out in this way, it's because I have felt slighted and, in turn, desire to hurt another. I want them to feel pain. I want to even the score, for them to realize their wrong and their need to change. I am not proud of behaving this way. It says more about my need to control than what wrongs may have been done to me. This is very unhealthy.

While my passive-aggressive tendencies get expressed in the intense way I send silent messages of disapproval to those I perceive as having slighted me, another form of passive-aggressiveness is evidenced in the person who "doesn't want to talk about it." Just the way these words are phrased makes it clear that the "it" is still unresolved. The words "I don't want to talk" make it equally clear that it will not be resolved.

Whose "Problem" Is the Problem?

If we focus on perceived slights, as Jerry Sola did in our road rage example, we give them power. If we let them fester into resentment or rage, we give them control over ourselves. An incident controls our "I am." Something takes over our "someone." As the clinical and social psychologist Dale Olen has noted, if people have a problem, it is their problem. When I allow their problem to be my problem, it *is* my problem. Only when I come to an understanding of the other who may have a problem will I be able to determine if I have a problem too![12]

This insight has been very helpful to me in addressing my anger issues. I have found it an aid in mitigating what, otherwise, might become a confrontation or even a blow-up between people. Here's how it worked for me in one instance.

A couple of years ago I was changing planes in Frankfurt for a flight to the United States. As I came to the area where I would be sitting I saw a man in a military uniform, already seated. As I placed my luggage in the overhead compartment above him, he gave me a "not too friendly" look. My first internal reaction was to say: "Do you have a problem?" But then I tried to envision my friend Dale Olen saying to me what he had written about whose problem "the problem" really was, at least as far as I was concerned: "Mike, you are making his problem your problem." So having let his advice invite me to an alternative response and having placed my luggage in the compartment, I closed the door and sat down nearby.

Almost as soon as I sat down I realized that I had forgotten something in my suitcase. I returned to retrieve the item from my luggage. Again, I got the dirty look from the military man. And, immediately, I almost blurted out: "Do you have a problem?" Thankfully the insight from Dale Olen captured my mind again and invited me to respond in a less confrontational way. I just said, "I'm sorry, sir, that I'm in your way. I'll finish as quickly as I can." This response disarmed him. He actually gave me something of a smile!

In a similar way, I have found that a "disarming" response to those who themselves would say to me, "What's your problem?" is simply to say: "I'm sorry." I don't need to tell them why I am sorry or what I'm sorry about. Their question is not an invitation to dialogue; it involves a demand that I change my thinking or behavior, so I just apologize. This disarms them and stops any dynamics of control from moving to deeper conflict.

Now we are ready to ask the question: What is the underlying foundation and nature of conflict in the first place?

Chapter Seven

Conflict: Its Sources and Debilitating Dynamics

"Those conflicts and disputes among you, where do they come from?" James wrote to the early Christians. "Do they not come from your cravings that are at war within you?" (James 4:1). James seems to be saying that if we have not been able to integrate our deepest sense of self with our human needs and desires, we end up being in conflict with others. Our conflicts with others indicate the presence of our own unresolved inner issues or struggles. Our ego needs/desires conflict with our "I am."

Building on James's insight, and if you are following the Power Chart, you will notice that conflict has two sources, as indicated by the arrows. Conflict arises as the consequence of the negative use of power around issues of control. However, not all conflicts come from destructive forces around us; they can also arise from simple misunderstandings among people who genuinely care for each other. This is revealed, for example, in the plea among conflicted parties in a marriage who say, "We really love each other and care deeply about each other, but we just cannot agree on _____." Such conflicts can be as simple as how to stack glasses in the dishwasher or cupboard or more complex, like questions related to the spending of money. At the heart of this kind of conflict, Nel Noddings writes, care still defines the relationship:

> Conflict may arise between the perceived need of one person and the desire of another; between what the cared-for wants and what we see as his best interest; between the wants of the cared-for and the welfare of persons yet unknown. We may even find ourselves in conflict between two persons for whom we care and whose interests and beliefs are incompatible. Sometimes, the conflict cannot be resolved and must simply be lived.[1]

At the individual level of life, the task of coming to maturity is to struggle through the various conflicts between opposing voices within and outside ourselves in such a way that we achieve some degree of integration between preserving our individuality and uniqueness and our need for interdependence and community. If psychologist Erik Erikson was right in his portrayal of the life journey, our conflict begins in childhood with the struggle to go beyond those voices that find us working out issues related to distrust and trust and, in the final stages of life, working through the conflict between despair and integrity and, finally, between stagnation and generativity.

As I worked on this book I read and heard about a conflict taking place beyond the "intrapersonal" level of life as articulated above. It took place on the interpersonal level. At a Chicago café called A Taste of Heaven, children were being allowed to roam freely, without parental guidance. Dan McCauley, the owner, posted a sign that read, "Children of all ages have to behave and use their indoor voices when coming to A Taste of Heaven." The sign provoked umbrage in some parents, who felt the sign implied criticism of how they handled their children. Soon whispers of a boycott passed among the young professional families moving into the hot real estate market where the café had located. "Really what they're saying is they don't welcome children; they want the child to behave like an adult," one complaining parent said.

As the conflict became more heated the press took notice. McCauley said the protesting parents were "former cheerleaders and beauty queens" who had "a very strong sense of entitlement." He distributed an open letter that warned of an "epidemic" of antisocial behavior. Then, in an interview with a reporter from the *New York Times* he addressed dynamics that speak to the core theme of this book: "If you send out positive energy, positive energy returns to you. If you send out energy that says I'm the only one that matters, it's going to be a pretty chaotic world." Then, making the connection to the bigger conflicts beyond his direct influence, he concluded: "I can't change the situation in Iraq, I can't change the situation in New Orleans [Hurricane Katrina]. But I can change this little corner of the world."[2]

Why do people find themselves in conflict? Why do dynamics that result in conflict in a café called A Taste of Heaven take place among religions that claim to know the way their adherents can enter heaven? Oftentimes, as our Power Chart illustrates, conflict is a consequence of one party's need to control another, who in turn rebels against this abuse. However, conflicts also result from some power-need not being met, affirmed, honored, and ensured. Unattended they can lead to further conflicts, increasing violence and, ultimately, breaks in the relationships in the form of divorce, strikes, and war among peoples.

The First Source of Conflict:
The Need to Control

The traditional interpretation of the serpent in the Garden of Eden reveals the source of all conflict in the world: the desire for power, in the form of control, as represented by the serpent, rather than accepting the power of God that makes us "good enough." Humanity has a need, from the beginning, to make everything conform to its tastes rather than God's vision of "good enough."

A popular commercial theme has been the "have it your way" at Burger King. In relationships, however, when one functions in ways that make it clear that he or she must "have it my way," conflict is inevitable. If these dynamics of control are not changed radically, they will easily lead to a breakdown in the relationship itself, be it a marriage, an office, or a nonprofit organization ordered to a common purpose.

I've met very few people who will be so honest as to say: "I want to control others." Rather, convinced that their way is the only way, they will exercise controlling dynamics in exploitative, manipulative, or coercive ways. The response on the part of those impacted by their negative use of power will be: "You don't really care; you're just trying to control."

We hear echoes of this statement when one spouse corrects the other, and when teenagers reproach their parents in the belief that the issue at hand has more to do with the parents' issues than the good of the youth. Such actions are often accompanied by the statement that thus-and-such is being done "for your own good"; in other words, it is an action based in care. But unless that care is consistent and observable it actually is hard to believe that correction will manifest forms of power other than control. I can say this from my own experience. Never, in all my backbiting toward my parents as a teen, did I ever accuse them of disciplining me from their own self-interest. Indeed, my mother's consistent care for me led me to believe her mantra as she proceeded to spank me when I was a child: "This hurts me more than it hurts you!"

Other echoes of the statement: "You don't really care; you're just trying to control" resound when people in other nations tell us about the selective way we, as a nation, seem to be willing to "defend" our interests. They pointedly ask why the United States was able to find it quite easy to invade Iraq on the pretext of saving the Iraqi people from a tyrant, but closed its eyes to the slaughter of hundreds of thousands of people in various parts of Africa at the very same time.

Variations of the statement also get expressed in the continual protests that surround gatherings of such international meetings of politicians and corporate executives as the World Economic Forum's annual meeting in Davos, Switzerland, meetings of the World Trade Organization and the Group of Eight, etc.

A Second Source of Conflict: Misunderstandings

Conflicts develop when individuals and groups that care about each other experience misunderstandings. If these conflicts are not resolved, manifestations of care can change quickly to dynamics of control. This makes it mandatory that we discover reasons why caring people can become quite at odds on this or that issue, even if their basic relationship may be grounded in otherwise caring dynamics. Basically, these kinds of conflicts take place because of misunderstandings.

Much misunderstanding in our relationships or among peoples occurs because of poor listening. How many times do we say to another who does not do our bidding: "Listen to me!" How many times do partners — whether lovers or parents with their children (and vice versa) say: "You're not listening to me!" The plaint of the teenager is often summarized in a few words: "You never listen to me." The same words mean "obey me" when parents say them.

What do we really mean when we use that phrase? It's not that the person is literally not listening to what we say; it really means that that person is not doing what we desire. This dynamic takes place in relationships when we *interpret* others' reality rather than *listen* to the way they want to articulate why they are the way they are, why they think or feel the way they do, or why they act in ways that may make us cringe.

Misunderstandings, especially when they are ongoing, follow a certain dynamic: the conflict arises from unresolved tensions between parties; the unresolved tensions flow from unrealized expectations and these unrealized expectations occur because of assumptions we have made independently but have not shared or agreed upon. The process can be charted as follows:

UNAGREED ASSUMPTIONS → UNREALIZED EXPECTATIONS →
UNRESOLVED TENSIONS → MISUNDERSTANDINGS → CONFLICT

For instance, conflicts between parents and teenagers about what time the child should return home hardly ever get settled, and the tensions between parents and child remain unresolved. Why? Both have different expectations about the proper hour a teen should return. Expectations deal with the "shoulds" of life, the "oughts" and the "musts" (as well as the should nots, the ought nots, and the must nots). Parents demand one time; the child holds out for another. Why are these expectations not realized? Both parents and child operate from different assumptions about what can happen beyond parental or societal curfews. The parents know from their own experience that things can go wrong and are distrustful that good can occur after hours. Teens believe and trust that they will do the right thing (or, if they know they will do the wrong thing, they trust they won't get caught or hurt). The result: an impasse.

If the parents resort to the imposition of control, negativity will define the decision. They will not be happy with how the decision was reached, and the teen will be angry about it.

How, then, do such conflicts get resolved among people who do, otherwise, deeply care for each other? And how can such parties to a potential conflict find ways to avoid any "war" that might ensue if the conflict does not get resolved except through conflict maintenance and the control by the more dominant party in the relationship (i.e., the parent, team leader, or "boss")? I will address the positive approaches to resolution in the chapter on collaboration; for now it is important to note that misunderstandings need not remain dead-end impasses.

A Key Source of Conflict among Groups: Unequal Power Relationships

Earlier I noted how unequal power relationships among social groups are abusive. However, as in domestic abuse, the victim will remain a victim until she (as is the usual case) realizes such behavior is not acceptable or "her fault." Historically, conflicts between groups arise because of the victimized group's increasing consciousness that they are in an unequal power relationship that must be changed. Until that happens they will be influenced by a certain way of thinking among those who benefit from the unequal power arrangements. In fact, many times it will be assumed that such disordered configurations constitute the only way a group can function. Sometimes, as with "Americanism," its adherents will believe the social arrangements are even divinely sanctioned.[3] I have called this way of thinking "ideology."

Anthony Giddens writes that there are three main forms of legitimizing this kind of negative ideology. The first represents one's group interests as universal. A second is found in a denial of any differences. A third is what he calls a "reification," or objectifying, normalizing, or making "natural" the present social arrangements. While Giddens does not say that such stances are consciously embraced in order to dominate, manipulate, coerce, or control others, he does say that such dynamics are ensured because of differential power dynamics.[4]

Until victimized people recognize the abuse done to them as abuse, they will remain passively submissive to those intent on keeping them controlled. That is why education can be so enlightening among some dominated groups and why their *conscientization* (or coming to empowerment through education) can be so threatening, as it was with African Americans in the United States in the civil rights period, and considered by those in power to be subversive, unpatriotic, and disloyal. When these groups of people are not recognized or acknowledged in their grievances, their organizing and uprising or civil disruptions to draw attention to their plight will be considered a "riot" rather than a rebellion against unjust and, therefore, unequal power relationships. When women began demanding equality with men at all levels and their efforts were rebuffed, they were often called "radical feminists" who "just want power." It is this language of dismissal that is a pervasive tactic to preserve unequal power relationships in social arrangements.

At a certain point in such an unequal context, such violence will likely beget violence.

Chapter Eight

Violence in Our Lives,
Groups, and World

My approach has been deeply influenced by two operating definitions. The first is that "power" itself is "the ability to influence." Everything in our lives and relationships (marriages and families, workplace dynamics and group work, as well as institutions and their governance) will reflect underlying power dynamics that work for good or harm. When those power dynamics result in harm they do so because of the exercise of forms of control that are sustained through fear and intimidation. A consequence of this is that someone will be hurt or abused.

This led to our second operating definition, that of abuse itself. I defined abuse as any way one uses to control others through fear or intimidation. These others can be individuals, groups, or institutions. People who are dominated, manipulated, or exploited are often afraid to challenge their abusers because of the way the abusers exercise power. The consequence is increasingly destructive relationships, more and more conflicts, and, if not checked, more and more violence.

This leads me to a working definition of violence. Violence is "any (un)intentional force that inflicts injury, hurt, or abuse." If abuse is any way one uses to control through fear or intimidation, and if control is the negative use of power, violence ultimately results from a chain of negative power dynamics in our relationships as individuals, groups, and peoples.

My interpretation of violence as a consequence of the negative use of power that is grounded in the need to control and that results in abuse differs from the understanding of violence that has been de rigueur in many circles in the recent years. This is found in the theory of "mimetic" desire — wanting the same object as another and competing for it — articulated by René Girard and popularized by Gil Bailie in his book *Violence Unveiled*.[1] Other writers such as Robert Hamerton-Kelly[2] and Richard Rohr[3] have taken the ideas of Girard and Bailie further into the realm of theology. Without going into detail on their writings but highly recommending them to the interested reader, I want to point out the ways in which I differ in my analysis of violence.

While there is a certain "elegance" to Girard's theory, I find it problematic insofar as he never defines violence, as I have done in this book. Once violence is defined we find it in, among, and around us, not just "out there." Neither does Girard adequately offer a way of preventative nonviolence, except a vague assurance that, when violence ends, right order will be (re)established. Neither do I feel that Girard adequately deals with the day-to-day ways we use and abuse power individually, communally, and collectively. While we descendants of those who hunted down witches in Salem continue to find scapegoats in women and homosexuals, I believe we do so more out of fear of that which is merely different than as a result of mimetic desire. Furthermore, the way Christians since the first centuries after Jesus' sacrificial death have dealt with their conflicts indicates they still have not learned from past religious wars, nor have they stopped the verbal violence around him whose way of "salvation" is truly salvific.

I also do not believe all conflicts necessarily lead to violence. This is evident in the success people and groups have in resolving conflicts through mediation rather than escalating tensions. Finally, I believe the fact that a higher power or ideal, such as our understanding of God (or even such a notion as "the universal good") can always be invoked at any step in the process. In the grace of this God, truly whatever is right is possible.

Cultural Violence

After the April 2007 shooting deaths of thirty-two people at Virginia Tech, columnist Bob Herbert wrote a piece called "Hooked on Violence," in which he noted the large number of children and teenagers we lose regularly to gun violence. In the last twenty years, over a million people have been killed in the United States by firearms, more than the combined U.S. combat deaths in all the wars in all of the nation's history. He called this an addiction that must be acknowledged but continues to be swept aside: "Americans are addicted to violence, specifically gun violence. We profess to be appalled at every gruesome outbreak of mass murder ... but there's no evidence that we have the will to pull the guns out of circulation, or even to register the weapons and properly screen and train their owners."[4]

Violence in the United States takes many forms and seems to have become the very environment within which we breathe. This is especially true of those who have been nurtured in climates of fear and intimidation as well as poverty and marginalization. Thus, in my city of Milwaukee, a defense lawyer could argue on behalf of her thirteen-year-old client, who had been involved in the murder of a visiting nurse who was caring for her grandmother, that she was suffering from "urban psychosis."[5]

But such violence is not limited to our inner cities, and never was. When Colorado suburban high school students Dylan Klebold and Eric Harris killed some of their classmates and themselves, people were shocked, in part because these boys came from above-average families. Attempting to understand how this could happen, columnist Peggy Noonan wrote an op-ed piece that I find to be one of the finest articulations ever written explaining the character of the violence in this nation. In noting that people were searching for explanations, she offered:

> Here's mine. The kids who did this are responsible. They did it. They killed. But they came from a place and a time, and were yielded forth by a culture.
>
> What walked into Columbine High School Tuesday was the culture of death. This time it wore black trench coats. Last time it was children's hunting gear. Next time it will be some other costume, but it will still be the culture of death. That is the Pope's phrase: it is how he describes the world we live in.

At that Noonan moves to a metaphor about the pervasiveness of this "culture of death":

> The boys who did the killing, the famous Trench Coat Mafia, inhaled too deeply the ocean in which they swam.
>
> Think of it this way. Your child is an intelligent little fish. He swims in deep water. Waves of sound and sight, of thought and fact, come invisibly through that water, like radar: they go through him again and again, from this direction and that. The sound from the television is a wave, and the sound from the radio; the headlines on the newsstand, on the magazines, on the ad on the bus as it whizzes by — all are waves. The fish — your child — is bombarded and barely knows it. . . .
>
> This is the ocean in which our children swim. This is the sound of our culture. It comes from all parts of our culture and reaches all parts of our culture, and all the people in it, which is everybody.[6]

Noonan's linkage of violence with the "culture of death" invites us to deepen our analysis of the pervasiveness of violence in our culture and the systematized way it is sustained in our institutions and our "isms," and even canonized through an ideology that justifies "first strike" attacks against other nations who may differ from us or who pose a threat to our power goals and security interests.

Institutionalized Violence

Although I sensed the pervasiveness of this kind of violence, I never could put a name on it until I read something by Thomas Merton. After stating that the "real moral issue of violence" can easily be "obscured by archaic and mythical presuppositions," he wrote:

> We tend to judge violence in terms of the individual, the messy, the physically disturbing, the personally frightening. The violence we want to see restrained is the violence of the hood waiting for us in the subway or the elevator. That is reasonable, but it tends to influence us [i.e., have power over us] too much. It makes us think that the problem of violence is limited to this very small scale, and it makes us unable to appreciate the far greater problem of the more abstract, more global, more organized presence of violence on a massive and corporate pattern. Violence today is *white-collar violence, the systematically organized bureaucratic and technological destruction of man.*[7]

While Noonan addressed the violence in our own nation as being endemic to our very identity, it is clear that violence pervades the global reality as well. The last century was the most violent, in the number of those killed, of any period in history; 160 million people were killed by war, oppression, and genocide. Indeed, as William Vollmann demonstrated in 2003 with his 3,299-page opus on violence, it is ubiquitous as well as virtually inescapable. "If violence is a kind of dust that lies inside the house of the soul" of individuals and peoples, "there does not seem to be any way to sweep it out the door. We can only sweep it into one corner or another."[8] While I take Vollmann's point, I would assert that we can decide to close the door to violence in our own lives and work to reorder its negative roots in the way we work for nonviolent social change in our social relations and organizations.

Violence as Unjustifiable

In 1992, when the U.S. Catholic bishops realized they could not address the issue of "Women in the Church," because they would have to discuss their own use of fear and intimidation as leaders, they issued instead a statement on domestic violence. Some of their key points on domestic violence can be applied to violence at any level. The bishops updated this document a decade later. In both documents they declare in virtually the same terms: "Violence against women, in the home or outside the home, is *never* justified. Violence in any form — physical, sexual, psychological, or verbal — is sinful; many times it is a crime as well."[9]

Having worked out how violence results as I diagramed it on the Power Chart, the bishops' insight about violence has been very instructive as I consider the various forms and ideological justifications so many use to perpetuate violence in their relationships at all levels of life, whether in marriages and workplaces or in foreign policy decisions or the rules and regulations of religious groups, including the Vatican.

First of all, the bishops and most other commentators, such as William Vollmann in his massive examination of violence, insist that "most violence will always be unjustified."[10] Violence is, by and large, seen as a negative force, especially by its victims, but when it becomes normal, accepted, and even justified, the victim who eventually gains control can become the abuser. When this occurs violence is justified as the only way to keep effective control. Perhaps the classic historical example of this phenomenon is how the leaders of the once-persecuted Christians became the controlling group in Christendom. Where once they were known for refusing to bear arms, now, thanks to St. Augustine, a finely crafted "just war" theory was developed to be used and abused so that the abuse of the dominant group goes unquestioned. Might becomes right.

Violence always seems to be justified by the group that wields it. For instance, despite the fact that all major mainline denominations said the 2003 U.S. invasion of Iraq was "not justified," the majority of fundamentalist religious groups, along with the neoconservative spokespeople from the mainline denominations, developed quite sophisticated rationales as to why it could be justified.

Violence as Sinful

In their pastoral letter on domestic violence, the U.S. bishops note that "violence in any form — physical, sexual, psychological, or verbal — is sinful; many times it is a crime as well." This statement involves two parts: becoming aware of the many forms of violence, not just those articulated by the bishops, and the need to recognize violence as "sinful."

The bishops say that violence "in any form" is wrong. While they articulate two forms of violence that most people can easily identify — physical and verbal violence — they mention two other ways people can violate each other: sexual and psychological violence.

For years those articulating the cause of sexual abuse and violence in many relationships such as the family, the school, the church or synagogue, or the counseling room, have made it clear that such violence can take place because of a *prior* status of power belonging to the perpetrator. A mother can abuse her child because of the trust that child has in her. A priest in the Roman Catholic Church could abuse more easily because priests had unquestioned and unchallenged control over everyone in the parish. Teachers and counselors can use the inferior, needy status of a student or client precisely to accomplish sexual abuse. All sexual abuse in trusting relationships arises from a prior abuse of power.

While it's quite clear what sexual abuse or violence may be, psychological violence is not always so evident. We can easily find the scars that may come from physical violence, but psychological violence attacks the emotions and self-image rather than the body. That is because manipulation and coercion, which can be very subtle, are the main forms of psychological abuse or violence. Perpetrators of psychological violence make victims feel inferior through belittlement and condescension. These behaviors can be overpowering because the perpetrator makes the victim feel that she or he is wrong, while the abuser's behavior is justified. It is no wonder that many counselors insist that psychological violence is the most common form of abuse between spouses and between parents and children.

The U.S. bishops say that "violence in any form...is sinful." However, if we review our previously examined notion of original sin, and see "The Fall" as that action which resulted in violence, we can also say that such can also be called "original violence." Sin is fundamental violence against God, self, and others. It violates right relationships between God, others, and ourselves. When we respond to relationships in ways that are not right, Marjorie Hewitt Suchocki writes in *The Fall to Violence: Original Sin in Relational Theology,* there are cosmic consequences, since everything in my "I am" is interrelated and involves every other entity in creation itself:

> When, then, one responds to relation by violating the well-being of another, one has lessened the richness of experience not only for the other, but also for all (including the self) who exist interdependently with one another. Given the openness of interdependent existence,

it is impossible to violate one without having an effect upon all. Thus any single violation has communal effects. The same is true with regard to one's relation to the world of nature: To violate any aspect of the well-being of nature is to violate the well-being of all, including the self, who is interdependent with that aspect of nature. Every violation has individual and social effects. If one can presuppose that well-being is better than ill-being, then we can say that every violation is a rebellion against the well-being of creation.[11]

According to this way of thinking, violence is sin insofar as it refers to ways of relating that are harmful, in which one chooses the way of "the flesh" instead of the way that bears the fruit of the Spirit. In the process of such sin, be it individual, communal or collective, creation itself is diminished. When such behavior characterizes the members of the body of Christ, the behavior violates the integrity of the body itself.

The notion of violence as sinful is further understood when we adapt the language of the U.S. Catholic bishops regarding domestic abuse and violence in our homes and show how it is manifest in unequal power relationships in our structures as well. If violence is "any (un)intentional force that inflicts injury," is not illiteracy another form of violence? Should we be surprised when an article in the *San Francisco Chronicle* receives the title: "Layoffs Called One of the Biggest Causes of Violent Behavior"?[12] Or should it not be surprising that, in writing about these corporate layoffs, especially at the largest corporations, *Newsweek* would have a cover article featuring the CEOs of four large companies with mug-shots, as if they were criminals, under the title "Corporate Killers"?[13] Are not all these forms of economic violence, therefore, forms of social sin? Would it not be correct, then, to accompany a *Wall Street Journal* headline that reads: "As Rich-Poor Gap Widens in the U.S. Class Mobility Stalls," with a parallel headline that reads: "one more manifestation of our nation's underlying violence"? Or, when we read that the gap between the rich nations and the poor ones is increasing as well, that such news should be accompanied with the reminder that this represents "the sin of the world"?

But violence in all its forms is expressed, we have seen, in unequal power relationships within our nations in politics and economics and in our churches between men and women as well as clergy and laity. Thus when elitism and economic imperialism define access (or non-access) to power, should they not be named "sinful" when we recognize the fall-out from the abuse of power of those who have the control? Should not sexism and clericalism in our churches, especially one like the Roman

Catholic Church (whose leaders insist that such is the will of God), be called what it is: religiously sanctioned violence? Such a situation leads one to another form of religiously sanctioned violence: theological violence. This occurs when "God" is presented in a way that justifies unequal power relationships. When your theology serves unequal power relations in the institutional structure, and when that is justified by an ideological theology, it becomes idolatry. Idolatry is the first sin condemned in the commandments. Yet today, too many religions advocate dynamics that objective observers would classify as abominations and forms of idolatry because they reveal unacknowledged forms of violence.

Religiously Sanctioned Violence

Sometime before 9/11/01 I gave a parish retreat on Long Island. The coordinators hired a car to take me to the airport at the end of the retreat. I was not prepared, however, for the line of questioning addressed to me by the driver. "You're a priest, aren't you?" he asked. When I said I was, he asked, "Tell me, Father, what has been the primary source of more wars in our world than any other?" Surprised and, even more, unwilling to be baited, I said, "You are asking the question; I would think you believe you know the answer." Immediately he declared, "It's religion. Conflicts over religion have been the source of more violence in this world among peoples than any other source."

My first tendency was to be defensive, but instead I started to think of the various wars waged between the Greeks and Romans, reinforced by appeals to their gods, and how this evolved into wars between East and West, Islam and Christianity, Protestants and Catholics, Palestinians and Jews, Tutsi Catholics and Hutu Catholics, as well as Bosnians, Serbs, and Croats. I realized I better keep quiet!

Since then, especially in recent books that have defended atheism, one of the key arguments of the authors is the way religion has been used over the centuries, and continues to be used, to promote abuse and violence, terrorism and wars. It has also led me to probe more closely the notion of religiously sanctioned violence. At its core I find its adherents justifying their violence toward others on the basis of a warped notion of God that often is unconsciously promoted by their own religions. This becomes evident only when we see the more extreme forms of violence that take place in the name of the group's "gods."

As I was writing this book three incidents in my own nation revealed clearly how many people still worship a God who supports violence, murder, and mayhem. The first came when televangelist Pat Robertson declared that the stroke suffered by Ariel Sharon, then prime minister of Israel, was divine punishment for "dividing God's land."[14] The next came a day later, near my hometown of Fond du Lac, Wisconsin. At the funeral of Sgt. Andrew P. Wallace in nearby Ripon, a group of people from the Kansas-based Westboro Baptist Church hailed his death in Iraq, saying it was God's revenge on a country that accepts homosexuality. God, they said, was "punishing soldiers for defending a country that harbors gays."[15] The third came ten days later when the mayor of Katrina-devastated New Orleans said that the hurricanes that hit the nation in quick succession were a sign of God's anger toward the United States and toward black communities too, for violence and infighting. "God is mad at America," he said. These comments share a notion of a God who is violent — especially when we consider violence as "any force that inflicts injury" — and condones human acts of violence.

Along with Islam, the Judeo-Christian religions have not extricated their God from sanctioning and condoning violence. Rather than presenting a God who sees any form of violence as evidence of a breakdown in relationships, they invoke a God who authorizes violence toward those who they believe oppose the divine power. This is particularly manifest, I believe, in atonement theories that deal with salvation itself. Such theories became a matter of public discussion and debate in the controversy that surrounded the 2004 release of Mel Gibson's hugely successful movie *The Passion of the Christ*.

Now and then, however, people begin to realize that a God who demands violence and who sanctions it is not worthy to be God. One such person I encountered is Tommy Acosta of Chandler, Arizona. After watching Gibson's movie, he wrote his local paper an extended critique of a prevailing notion of salvation that underpins many of our ideas about redemption and salvation:

> I was taught that Christ died in order to wash away the stain of original sin acquired by Adam and Eve for disobeying God when they bit an apple from the Tree of Knowledge.
>
> I was stricken [watching the movie] with an unbelievable realization. I mean, what kind of a loving father allows such a thing to happen to their son and even worse, forgives disobedience through the murder of his own?
>
> Suddenly, none of what I was taught in school made sense anymore. God throws us out of the Garden of Eden, condemns us to pain, death, sorrow and anguish because we disobeyed by biting an apple, yet He forgives our original transgression when we murder

his son. Essentially, God had His own son sacrificed to appease himself!...

I will never be able to look at a Crucifix the same way again. Rather than a symbol of my religion, to me it now represents an instrument of torture and murder. Only through the shedding of His son's blood was God able to drop His anger toward us and forgive us. He condemns us for disobedience and forgives us through murder.

This is sick.... [16]

I agree with Mr. Acosta. Religion is sick when it creates a God who reflects human notions of act and response, tit for tat, and other forms of revenge, instead of nonviolent forms of reconciliation.

When we make our God sanction such violence, wars are justified "in God's name." Consequently morality canonizes murder. This tendency to justify or sanction violence with moral claims results in wars of all kinds.

While we refer to *war* on the Power Chart for times when conflicts and violence are not mitigated or eliminated, the word describes other breaks in our relationships too. So we have divorce in marriages, "breakups" of families, walk-outs and strikes between management and labor. Their moral justification offers an underlying attitude or ideology that can be invoked when an immediate cause becomes "the last straw."

Wars not resolved easily lead to the next stage: *hate.* One need only listen to talk radio to discover the incivility and downright meanness that people often exhibit when people with certain political, economic, or religious viewpoints discuss others who may differ with them. These "others" can easily become traitors, infidels, and the unsaved. Unaware of our own blinders, we become, in the eyes of these "others," a cause for their own hatred. Aware of this dynamic, Peggy Noonan wrote of such people who not only reject our U.S. ways but end up hating us: We often bring this hate on ourselves: "We make it too easy for those who want to hate us to hate us. We make ourselves look bad in our media, which helps future jihadists think that they must, by hating us, be good." [17]

When hate (with the other negative elements preceding it on our Power Chart) continues unabated, people and even institutions can easily move to *indifference;* they "do not care" what others think or believe, feel or act. Besides "not caring," other words for indifference are psychic numbing, compassion fatigue, hardness of heart, acedia, and anomie. Others make "no difference" to us, our communities, or our collective groupings. [18]

Chapter Nine

Recognizing the Need
to Change Our Way of Relating
in Our Use of Power

One of the most comforting teachings of Jesus is unique to Matthew's Gospel: "Come to me, all you that are weary and are carrying heavy burdens, and I will give you rest. Take my yoke upon you, and learn from me; for I am gentle and humble in heart, and you will find rest for your souls. For my yoke is easy, and my burden is light" (Matt. 11:28–30).

While many have found a paradox in the way power's consequences are described in relationships (i.e., weary/rest, heavy/easy, burden/light), I am finding much of what I am saying in this book about the paradox of power and its expression on the Power Chart revolving around two images used in the sentences above that deal with the "I am" of Jesus and our own souls, our unique "I ams."

My interpretation of the passage is twofold: we are under the yoke of control in ways that have created weariness, heaviness, and burdens for ourselves (and others); and, secondly, we have "learned" that this relates to ways that have brought these negative results of the abuse of power. The hope contained in the passage is also twofold: there is another way of using power that need not create negativity and, secondly, that we must learn this from the way Jesus used power. The consequence is clear: we must convert to the degree that we stop using power in ways that yoke negatively and take on the yoke, the power-dynamics of Jesus. This demands that we unlearn what we have been taught by the ideology of our prevailing culture and religion and embrace the true teachings about power that we find in the Jesus of the Gospels.

What makes us realize that we have been functioning under a yoke of control that has made us and others "weary"? What makes us realize that we have had laid on our shoulders "heavy burdens" and have done the same to others? What makes us able to finally hear the invitation of Jesus to use our God-given power in another way — to "come to" his way of using power and to "learn from" him a way of using power that is nonviolent and that will make ourselves and others much more at rest?

Psychologist Erik Erikson believed that every human being experiences at least eight major crossroads in a lifetime. As we grow through the stages of life from childhood to old age, the signs that we may be at another juncture in our life can be signaled in depression, anxiety, lack of energy, disturbed sleep, or mood disturbances. Some of the decisions that we consequently make in these situations can be major, life-changing events.

In other instances, life changes can occur because of a compelling sense that one can make a significant contribution to the lives of others. I know of a man in Louisville who was on the fast track to become an executive in General Electric. After some chance encounters with inner city youth he felt impelled to change careers and get enough credits and accreditation to become a high school teacher. At crossroads like this, according to Ray Bender, a Milwaukee-area psychiatrist, "one can look back on what's happened in life either as a positive or a negative"[1] and then choose to continue on the path that has been taken if that is perceived to be a positive direction or choose to change if one comes to realize the existing way one has lived is not healthy or helpful.

While such transformative moments and consequent responses to them seem to be normal, what happens when we reach a crossroad not regarding our personal development, but rather the need to develop healthier and more constructive relationships with others? What happens when we realize that the way we have been relating has been negative rather than positive? What dynamics make us begin to realize we cannot continue to relate to people who may be very close to us in the way that we have been?

The Decision to Change the Way We Use Power in Our Personal Relationships

Every person lives in two worlds: an outer world and an inner world. The outer world often is that defined by the dynamics of the first level of our Power Chart. The inner world represents the core of my "self," my "I am." The process of maturation and transformation from a life path of violence to compassion involves becoming more fully aware of the negative dynamics within us represented in the top part of the chart and to create a way of life, with others, that will enable us to work on the positive dynamics represented in the bottom part of the chart.

How does this happen?

First of all we must recognize how those who have abused their power have taken our power away from us and that we must recapture it. "Living from a position of power must be learned," the authors of *The Dynamics of Power* write. Consequently, we must find ways to maintain "equal power in relation to others whenever possible." This demands a nurturing of skills needed to name the reality and dynamics that take place in ways that have overpowered us. They say: "Once we are aware of our helplessness we can name it consciously to ourselves: 'I am feeling powerless,' or 'I am so damn enraged over feeling helpless.' The next step is to consciously observe the situation to see where and how we can take back the power."[2] Notice that the authors do not say that we should look for ways to take back the "control," but take back the "power."

Secondly we must recognize how we have used power in ways that have taken it from others. In my own life the realization that I had come to live on the top part of the chart came after frustrations with increasing conflicts I encountered with another powerful (i.e., influential) person in my community. I believed in a certain way to exercise influence — control — and he rebelled against my forms of manipulation and domination. On the other hand, I got my "back up" at the way he tried to keep me from reaching my goals. Ultimately, I found that the *way I was using my power — by control —* was actually undermining my goal of influencing the members of the community. I realized I had to change before I invited others to change. Furthermore, I realized the way I had been challenging others to change was not effective.

When I finally realized that I had been using power in a way that was destructive and undermining my attempts to bring about the change I so desired, especially in my efforts to influence coworkers to change their working style or people close to me to commit to social change (and to my way of effecting it and my ideas of what it would look like), I realized I had to change; otherwise I would only be reinforcing the very control, abuse, conflict, and violence that I purportedly saw in others (in need of change) but not in myself.

Once we become free of others' control and then realize how we have done the same to others, we now are ready to engage in a life path of compassion. The key here, whether we are speaking of ourselves as individuals, groups, or members of institutions interrelating with others, is that all our relating must be to share *equal power* with others so that all involved are energized and empowered rather than de-energized and overpowered. Thus, in a one-on-one relationship of power, it becomes a resource that gives me half and you half. To want more than that violates the relationship. Spiritually, such would be untrinitarian and ungodly.

In our personal relationships, when affirmation and correction flowing from that affirmation define a relationship, there is created a kind of "envelope of care" or "holding environment." We must develop relationships in which any kind of challenge or correction we make to others must first flow from our affirmation of them and their experience of that dynamic of affirmation. This has become a central conviction of my life — especially in those areas where I find myself trying to invite others to change the way they think, feel, or act.

Indeed, I have learned this the hard way. In the past I found it easy to correct but not to affirm. As a result, people developed their own coping mechanisms to be free of my various forms of manipulation and exploitation, coercion and domination.

My realization of this began with my way of trying to influence my group to change by becoming more radically involved in social justice. In my effort another member of the group to which I still belong opposed me — not in my ends but in my means. His name is Matthew Gottschalk.

Like myself, my group has considered Matthew Gottschalk to be an influential person, i.e., a "power person." Unlike myself, Matthew was not operating out of dynamics of the need to control anyone, including the group. Matthew was very actively involved in the need for social change; indeed, he had received a master's degree in sociology. He had marched with Dr. Martin Luther King Jr. in Selma and Montgomery, Alabama. He represented our group of brothers at King's funeral in Atlanta. So Matthew was very knowledgeable and involved in social change.

Aware of the dynamics of group change and the way we can use our influence vis-à-vis groups in positive or negative ways, Matthew did not like it when he saw other persons (like myself) using their power to try to control the group, even if we agreed on the goals related to social change. When he saw me and the small group of which I was a member operate he often resisted. He felt a need to turn us in a positive direction. While we called ourselves the "Movers and Shakers," he and many of the other brothers saw that we functioned in another way that they would call the "Manipulators." Consequently, when one of us would present an idea that would *demand* change on the part of the group, Matthew would go to the podium to argue against it. At that I would get my "back up." The result: Matthew "pushed back" in reaction to my way of using power, and I got my "back up" when he "pushed back." There was a standoff.

One time I wrote a paper outlining our social reality as a group. I challenged the brothers in the group to change. The consequence was that 250 brothers got their collective "backs up." And then it hit me: Matthew gets his "back up" when he sees how I challenge; I get my "back up" when Matthew does this, and now the whole group gets its collective "back up" when I challenge it and try to get it to correct its ways of functioning.

Why do we get our "backs up?"

I have discovered that most positive people like Matthew Gottschalk have a "Michael Crosby" in their lives. For me, vis-à-vis Matthew, I got my "back up." But other people react with body language that warns them of the danger that is impending when someone is trying to control them. Some get sweaty palms, others find their stomachs churning, while still others find their jaws protrude or body stiffening. Some feel a deep desire to flee. Other reactions, not always felt, can occur as well, like one's eyes getting set or one's face becoming flushed. Why? We feel invaded. Our boundaries have been violated. The sense of being attacked makes us viscerally ordered to "protect" and "defend" ourselves; we feel threatened and insecure. Thus the defenses we build to save ourselves from the attacker, the potential violator.

Correction without Care Is Control

When I realized I had contributed mightily to being in relationships where many of us were "walking around with our backs up," I also realized nothing was changing as a result. Everyone was being defensive. For my part, I was challenging Matthew and others, but my challenge was not based on care. It was at that time that a saying came to me. The five-word sentence has changed my life — and, I hope, the way I try to relate: "Correction without care is control."

To challenge others without first confirming them in their own self-worth, be they individuals, groups, or members of institutions, will be experienced by those others as control and uncaring. When we function this way, when we use our power in this negative way in a relationship, the only response for a healthy person will be to become defensive. When we want to correct or challenge others, if those others do not experience this invitation to change as coming from care and respect, they will create walls to defensively protect themselves from our invasive actions.

Dale Olen, with doctorates in both clinical and social psychology, writes: "Years ago I heard the phrase 'carefronting.' When differences appear, you want to 'carefront' the other rather than 'confront.' "[3] If confrontation is a form of control, carefronting is a manifestation of care. Our "front" toward the other with whom we differ must be care rather than control.

So what are we to do? We want to change structures; we want to challenge people to change. We want to be effective. We don't want to waste our time. We want to be successful in our exercise of power. However, if we use our influence in such a way that it is perceived or experienced as negative and overpowering, the automatic reality for those on the receiving end will be defensiveness. The only way they will come under your controlling ways is if they happen to be in structured relationships where they depend on you for their survival or security.

All this has convinced me that all authentic relationships, if they are going to energize all the members, must be grounded in dynamics of affirmation from which any correction will follow. When this occurs, care will be the result. As I have changed, I have found that those who used to employ defenses in relation to me have begun their own disarming. If all life is relational and if all relationships of significance involve power, when negative power is reoriented to what builds up a relationship, the others being affected by positive power are energized to react in positive ways: we become tuned to the same wavelength in harmony one with the other.

What Adult Have You Ever Changed?

A second insight that is helping free me from my tendency to control and overpower others (and, I hope, has made me easier to be with) is to ask the question, "What adult have you ever changed?" When I give workshops, I often pose this to the participants. To this day, not one person has acknowledged being able to *make* another adult change his or her life.

Just as I learned from Matthew, when we are free in our lives and relationships, we will not be open to correction or challenge unless we feel they are coming to us from care. I also have learned from my interactions with others who have tried to change me through negative force. I will not change unless I decide to, again, if I am truly free. Given the situation, some people and some institutional representatives may be able to control my behavior, but nobody can make me really change unless I decide to change. In cases when I must submit to their controlling ways, I may submit to their authority or abuse but I will do so only under duress, fear, or intimidation. Outwardly they may control my behavior, but inwardly they will not control my mind. As the young girl said to her teacher who told her to "sit down" after the student challenged him about something he had said: "I may have to sit down with my body, but in my spirit I'm still standing up."

Once a review of my adult life and its changes reveals that nobody but myself has made me change, I am more ready to accept the fact that neither can I change people. When I truly grasp this insight, I begin to act differently toward them, especially if I truly want to influence their thinking and acting. This makes me realize that I have every right to try to influence them by offering them my ideas or even challenging their thinking or behavior. However, now I try to relate to them differently as I do this, and I do so realizing I may or may not be heeded.

I do not think any person has the kind of power that makes another adult *really* change his or her life. Young people in grade school, high school, and college may have some truly significant teachers enter their lives as role models or have taken courses that they think "changed their lives." However, even in these situations, those teachers were more the occasion for us to see life differently in a way that invited us to make the changes necessary than the cause of such changes. The mentors and teachers did not change us; they used their power in ways that influenced us to change the way we thought, how we felt about things, and, sometimes, how we determined life choices, including our professions. But we made those decisions based on their influence, not on their control.

The Dynamics That Lead Us to Change the Way We Use Power

What happens to us in our personal journeys that invites us to move from the top of the Power Chart to the dynamics of a compassionate life path, I believe, should be able to be replicated at the level of groups and even nations.

For instance, in the late 1990s and early years of the third millennium, Liberia, the country to which many former slaves immigrated, was a case study in the various negative dynamics related to power and its abuse summarized on the top line of our Power Chart. But then something happened to the whole populace as illustrated by this 2005 *New York Times* story entitled "Youth Power in Liberia: From Bullets to Ballots":

> War took James Garmey's childhood. It came at night, in the form of armed men battering down a door and carrying him off, the eight-year-old son of a rural customs collector, to be a soldier for the warlord and future president Charles Taylor.

"I went to training," said Mr. Garmey, now twenty-two, speaking in the smooth patois of the Liberian street, letting consonants and bits of grammar slip away. "I was small, but I learned to hold gun and after a while went to battlefront. I fire gun; I defend my area."

When Mr. Taylor fled in 2003, Mr. Garmey finally put his gun down, saying he had traded it for a different weapon altogether: the ballot.

"I cast my vote and that is my power," he said. "I no need any more gun."[4]

One of the most beloved passages from the Hebrew Scriptures comes from the second chapter of the Book of Isaiah. In it "Judah and Jerusalem" (i.e., the "world" for the believer) were promised that another form of power would one day overcome the former power that had overwhelmed the people. God promised:

> In days to come the mountain of the Lord's house
> shall be established as the highest of the mountains,
> and shall be raised above the hills;
> all the nations shall stream to it.
> Many peoples shall come and say,
> "Come, let us go up to the mountain of the Lord,
> to the house of the God of Jacob;
> that he may teach us his ways
> and that we may walk in his paths."
> For out of Zion shall go forth instruction,
> and the word of the Lord from Jerusalem.
> He shall judge between the nations;
> and shall arbitrate for many peoples;
> they shall beat their swords into plowshares,
> and their spears into pruning hooks;
> nation shall not lift up sword against nation,
> neither shall they learn war any more.
> O house of Jacob,
> come, let us walk
> in the light of the Lord! (Isa. 2:2–5)

The hope in the passage above is that we can live in ways that use our power to move away from violence (our "swords") into nonviolence (our "plowshares"). Making swords or plowshares involves the use of power and various forms of energy. Everything depends on how we use our power and direct our energy: it will continue to be done in negative ways or we will direct our power in alternative ways that bring about a new vision of reality. This demands moving from former ways of darkness into "the light of the Lord." It demands embracing a way of conversion.

In every great spirituality, conversion involves the process of moving from one way of relating that is either personally, communally, or collectively negative to embrace another way of life that is positive. We never will move from one way of relating to another unless we recognize either that the negative consequences of continuing in one way of life are too great or that the positive consequences of embracing another way of life are too desirable. For whatever reasons this "conversion" takes place, we "let go" of dynamics of control and move into a way of care in our individual lives, in our relationships, and in our institutions. Our universe can only be better (more healthy) as a result.

The passage from Isaiah about turning or "converting" our swords into plowshares also assumes that this can be accomplished when the People of God allow God and God's ways to become theirs. When we finally realize how we have been living with swords rather than plows in our personal, communal, and collective relationships, we become more willing to turn our spiritual selves over to God's power or reign so that God's messianic power is released in us. As the Serenity Prayer so eloquently states it: "God grant me the serenity to accept the things I cannot change, the courage to change the things I can, and the wisdom to know the difference."

When we connect with God's energizing power and learn to use our power in caring ways, we will be on our way to embark on the path of compassion as outlined on the lower half of our Power Chart.

Chapter Ten

The Constituents of Care

Who/What Can Care?

For years I have thought that the Power Chart is applicable to all levels of relationships in the world: personal, communal, and institutional or organizational. In many ways I want to still believe that if these levels of life represent human relationships, they should be humane and, therefore, moral or ethical. So ideally I stand by my conviction: the most basic meaning of human existence is to create cultures of care.

This made me think of my own institution, the Roman Catholic Church, and the data from so many English-speaking countries in the "North" that indicate that the "church" seemed more concerned about preserving its institutional identity than the well-being of its most vulnerable members. Or, looking at what happened in Poland, the same parallels seemed to be operative: Did the hierarchy knowingly close its eyes to collaboration with the Communists by some of its key clerics even as it publicly presented another face? Or, when we look at patriarchal forms of governance in parts of sub-Saharan Africa, is the church immune from the abuse of women, including nuns, by members of its clergy (including bishops) in some of those countries?[1]

Can the church be moral when, organizationally, data continually show that it seems more concerned with maintaining the survival of a small group of its male, celibate clergy at the expense of its constituents' participation in its life, including their ability to regularly celebrate the Eucharist, its core-identifier? The question arose in my mind: Can such an organization really "care"? Can this kind of a "what" care?

Given her understanding of care as the key ingredient of ethical relationships, Nel Noddings insists that "organizations cannot be ethical." Of all organizations she writes: "They demand loyalty, insist upon the affirmation of certain beliefs, and separate members from nonmembers on principle." However, having said that, she moves on to discuss why she believes religious institutions (for me, the institutional expression of the Roman Catholic Church, which often seems to be recognized as a "what" more than a "who") can so easily be unethical:

> Even religious organizations often tend to diminish the ethical ideal. They take a special responsibility of the moral education of their members and, especially, that of the young. Often they do effectively immunize the young against certain conventional immoralities ... but they seem to be notoriously ineffective in preventing the great, fatal ills. Indeed, it must be acknowledged that they often contribute to these great ills. Cruelty and harsh judgment are not strangers to religion. Further, the frequent insistence on obedience to rules and adherence to ritual contributes to the erosion of genuine caring. One is led to seek self-preservation in the form of salvation. Even the precious other — he who defines me in human relation — becomes an instrument of my salvation. If the church wills it, I behave benevolently toward him and win stars in my crown; if the church wills it, I destroy him and, again, find my reward in paradise.

Given the place of "freedom" as an expression of care, along with trust (which must be in place), if we are to construct healthy relationships at all levels of life including our institutions, I would agree with the first part of Noddings's conclusion below and hope that we might also find a way to have an institution whose members share its core beliefs — precisely because they have been involved in the creation of those core beliefs. Noddings puts it this way: "Only if the church allows and promotes unlimited freedom of caring can it be an instrument of ethicality. Then it becomes a collection of persons who share an attitude and a commitment...."[2]

Acknowledging the Overpowering Role of Fear in Our Relationships

If indifference or apathy is the ultimate consequence of an uncaring life, care or empathy is the starting point for us to use our power to make a difference in our relationships at all levels of life. Genuine care stands as polar opposite to indifference; in fact, as its Gothic root *kara* means, it is a lament at all that is wrong in our world; it is a cry against dynamics like those on the top part of our Power Chart. So if we are to commit ourselves to using our caring power, we must first rid ourselves of fear in our lives to open our energy, our lives toward trust and freedom.

Interestingly enough, "Be not afraid" appears in one form or another 365 times in the Bible.[3] President Franklin Delano Roosevelt in his "Four Freedoms" speech to the nation at a time of domestic crisis and impending war against Germany spoke as inspiringly as his voice would allow over the radio to his fellow countrymen: "We have nothing to fear but fear itself." He too meant *every single day of the year* "Be not afraid."

Psychologists tell us that the first step in realizing our full potential, or operating from a positive source of energy, occurs when we have the courage to face our fears directly rather than letting them control us. In commenting on her decision to begin a talk show in Chicago, where Phil Donahue ruled the airwaves, Oprah Winfrey emphasized that "if you allow it to, fear will completely immobilize you." Consequently, she declared that the "true meaning of courage is to be afraid, and then, with your knees knocking and your heart racing," you step out:

> What I know for sure is this: Whatever you fear most has no power — it is your *fear* that has the power. The thing itself cannot touch you. But if you allow your fear to seep into your mind and overtake your thoughts, it will rob you of your life. Each time you give in to your panic, you will actually lose strength, while whatever you're afraid of will gain that strength. That's why the only real cure for fear is courage. You must decide that no matter how difficult the path ahead seems, you will push past your anxiety and keep on stepping.[4]

When we free ourselves of our own feelings of fear and intimidation we can begin to meet our true security needs. Building on our basic needs for relationality and power, we have other needs that will be met in a way that helps nurture in us and in our relationships and in the way we use power a distinctive "quality of caring." Embracing the conscious realization that we have basic needs for belonging, for touching and holding, for being part of a group that affirms and invites us to grow, we can experience ourselves opening up to others in a two-way relationship that validates and resonates with these needs in them as well.

That is why I have become convinced that caring is the basic requirement of every relationship of significance at all levels: personal, communal, and institutional, including the way nations relate to each other. "If we are ever to create a truly caring society, then we need people who know how to care and care deeply," Kaufman and Raphael write. "We need people who care about people, social conditions, our environment, and our future. We must value caring and teach people how to care just as we teach them how to live with a sense of power in their lives. Caring is the soul of human vulnerability and the soil from which we spring."[5]

Before any of us can be a part of or construct a healthy community of trust, we must face fear head on. Those who live by creating fear in us do so as their means of control; by refusing to be bullied and overwhelmed in anxiety about when they might next strike, our unwillingness to come under their control takes power from them. We can take as our model the peace activist Eileen Egan, as described in *Parade* magazine. Even though, at eighty-two, she was mugged and took a year to recover, she declared: "I refuse to live in fear." She would not succumb to become a victim of those who had perpetrated the violence against her. And, to do what she could to keep herself from entering the cycle of violence in her world she decided to become an advocate for prisoners "to turn away from violence. . . . "[6] She continued using her caring power in this creative way until her death in 2000.

Care: The Minimum Requirement of All Constructive Relationships

In our culture we distinguish among relationships defined by loving, by liking, and by caring. I don't think the average person can love all people (especially given so much polarization in our culture), and I believe we cannot like many types of people. However, I am becoming absolutely convinced that, if people and the planet are to survive, care must define all our relationships with both, and that care must not show favoritism between people and the planet since both of these "others" are necessary for our own survival.

If power is never neutral but either a force for help or harm that energizes or de-energizes, and if our way of influencing each other is grounded in ways that overpower or empower each other, then care, simply speaking, is the minimal requirement for all relationships that we consider to be positive, right, or good. Since all relationships involve power, how we relate and influence one another in our relationships is critical if we are to have positive, right, and good ways of being with each other. Since care in the form of respect is the core requirement for such relationships, care constitutes the heart of the human condition, if our relationships are going to be constructive at all levels, including those in society itself. Our "first and unending obligation," therefore, is to meet the other as a person who cares.[7]

In her book *Caring,* Nel Noddings defines all constructive relationships as involving care in a way that involves the "one-caring" and the other as the one "cared-for." She writes: "Taking relation as ontologically basic simply means that we recognize human encounter and affective response as a basic fact of human existence. As we examine what it means to care and to be cared for we shall see that both parties contribute to the relation; my caring must be somehow completed in the other if the relation is to be described as caring."[8]

Noddings points to negative dynamics (such as those that I have previously discussed on the Power Chart), noting that, when these various ways of relating define our relationships, such ways of relating will be unethical and, therefore, not right and not good. This is because the other is treated not with dignity and respect but as one who is devalued and, therefore, able to be treated "differently." But an "ethic of caring" does not permit such behavior to define the way we relate at any level:

> Our ethic of caring will not permit this to happen. We recognize that in fear, anger, or hatred we will treat the other differently, but this treatment is never conducted ethically. Hence when we must use violence or strategies on the other, we are already diminished ethically. Our efforts must, then, be directed to the maintenance of conditions that will permit caring to flourish.[9]

When care defines our relationships we are concerned when the other experiences any of the negative elements on the top part of the chart. In effect, the "other" is able to make a claim on my "I am." Thus we can say, in such negative situations, "I am concerned" rather than "I don't care." At the same time, we are not just concerned about others insofar as they may be experiencing any of the debilitating (and "uncaring") elements on the top part of the chart; we find ourselves desiring the good for them, wanting to create the kind of environment in which they will be able to be respected, honored, and cared for by others besides ourselves. As Noddings writes, "Our motivation in caring" in this way "is directed toward the welfare, protection, or enhancement of the cared-for."[10]

Grounding All Power Relationships in Care via Mutual Affirmation and Correction

We all know care when we experience it in our relationships; it is the power that empowers and energizes us. All positive power in any and all relationships is, first of all, constituted in care. Since our definition of power is "the ability to influence," when care defines how we use that influence, we empower others to find their best selves, to feel welcome, and to create institutions and social dynamics that build a healthier world.

Blaine Lee, founding vice president of the Covey Leadership Center, writes:

> The person you believe is powerful is someone others believe in, someone they honor, someone they respect. They comply with this person's wishes because they want what she wants. Whether she is there or checking upon them or paying them does not matter. She believes in them and they believe in her. As a consequence, people willingly and wholeheartedly give themselves over to what she asks of them. This person has power *with* others, not over them.[11]

While I find much in Lee's approach very helpful, am convinced that a change in our behavior leads to a change of heart. He believes the opposite. His approach is based on principles, not practices or, as he insists: "If you understand principles, you can create effective practices."[12] The way I see it is if you act on your basic principles about relating to people with power by honoring them, you will change in the process. In the end, it may involve a "both/and" rather than an "either/or."

Having learned from others who have shown me care in ways that meet my basic needs, I have become absolutely convinced that manifestations of genuine affirmation followed by correction are essential in every relationship of significance. Healthy affirmation is the stuff that makes people feel respected and of significance. It must ground all subsequent corrections, challenges, and confirmations when they are deemed necessary for good human development and differentiation. However, any such correction or challenge to another person must be packaged in a way in which the one being challenged is, first-of-all, affirmed and honored. This is what Donald Winnicott calls the "envelope of care."[13]

I got a sense of the two styles people use to correct (in constructive or destructive ways) from some friends of mine who are grandparents. Morgan is the grandson of Tom and Darlene White. When he was little they talked almost every day. Once a week Morgan would stay at their home. Somehow, it seems, when Tom felt the need to correct Morgan he often began to pout. But it didn't happen when Darlene did the challenging. "Why the difference?" I asked. "I don't know exactly what Tom does that generates Morgan's sadness," Darlene said. "But before I ever correct him, I say: 'Morgan, Grandma wants you to come here a minute.' When he comes I hold him in my arms. Then I kind of rock him. And when I can sense he is feeling safe, I talk with him."

When affirmation followed by correction characterizes the use of power, the relationship will be grounded in care. Care is the positive use of power. As such, it is the minimum requirement of every relationship of significance. Care must be the context for all connectedness in the universe, at every level of life. Since no relationship is neutral, when care does not constitute relationships at the individual, interpersonal, or institutional levels, the dynamics in those relationships will be abusive, hurtful, or alienating. This demands an attitude of openness rather than critique as we approach those who are different from us or who differ with us. Since the way we perceive others affects the way we relate to them, to start from negative impressions will lead inevitably to negative consequences.

In my own life, I will no longer live in community with others unless we can agree to the "higher power" of some kind of "ground rule" that revolves around affirmation and correction in ways that will nurture the dynamics of care among us. In my mind, this is the sine qua non of every marriage, communal form of living, and, I would add, every core group whose members interact with each other on a regular basis. The nurturing of care is something that must begin as early as possible, even in the womb, and be cultivated with babies in the way we communicate with them. Affirmation can never end until, and even after, the tomb.

My work and living is defined by a small group of people. We have agreed on one way that we will relate: we will affirm each other and be open to be affirmed; from this affirmation we will be open to be corrected and to correct each other. This affirmation and correction provide the character of our group functioning.

Such a ground rule cannot be assumed as a "given" in any relationship; it must be stated and restated. Many people think that, because they are married, such a way of relating comes with the terrain. But it is not contained in the wedding vows or with the contract for working in this or that place. You have to negotiate and create a dynamic for this to happen. Normally, it has to be written down or accepted in some way. Otherwise, if one assumes she or he can be connected to the other by affirming and correcting and the other has not agreed upon this assumption, you will have the potential for conflict and, possibly, a break in the relationship.

The Freedom to Be and to Grow in Trust

When people find themselves in such a setting of mutually agreed-upon affirmation and correction two things happen: people mutually feel they can be free to say what they think and feel, and from this, be free to be "who I am." Indeed the ultimate freedom of all people, precisely because of the dignity they have been endowed with by their Creator, is to say of themselves, as this Creator has also said: "I am who I am."

I believe that, even where and when dynamics of control have disempowered people and any resulting trust may have been compromised or even eroded, once we discover our core identity as persons who are free to be our true and, therefore, best *selves* and work to realize this in our relationships through mutual affirmation and correction, we can begin to heal the hurts of the dynamics that might have reflected elements of the top part of the Power Chart and, at the same time, begin to empower each other through a renewed commitment of care.

If nature and nurture are the two main determinants of our character, when our core relationships are grounded in care, care becomes the most powerful positive form of nurturing (re)energized relationships at all levels.

Years ago I was impressed by the title of a book: *Why Am I Afraid to Tell You Who I Am?*[14] I now don't recall anything I read from it, but, given our Power Chart, I've discovered that where dynamics of control in the form of fear and intimidation define a relationship, persons who are fear-based or fear-responsive never feel free to say what they think or feel; they are afraid to say who they are. As a result their freedom is compromised; their uniqueness is dishonored. In the process, their "I am" gets objectified as something to be manipulated and exploited, coerced, or dominated. A consequence easily can become anger.

On the other hand, when people feel free to talk about what has made their "I am" to be what it is — their lives, their past experiences and embarrassments, their present thoughts and feelings, and their future hopes and expectations in an environment of care — they become free from the fear of any shame that might be involved in doing so. Since fear cancels out freedom, the more people feel free to be who they truly are — an empowered person rather than an overpowered person or overpowering person — the less fear will define their "I am" and the way they relate. The resulting relationship with the other in his or her "I am" will help overcome any debilitating fears and engender ever deepening levels of trust between and among them.

However, freedom is more than a freedom *from* the forces of control; if it is a manifestation of care, it must be a force in relationships that is personal and interpersonal. In other words, my freedom cannot compromise the freedom of others.

Although we in the United States define ourselves as living in the "land of the free," we often have been manipulated by politicians and corporate executives who abused their power through intimations that our freedom may be threatened. We seemed quite willing to come under their control once they convinced us that our freedom was at stake. Edward Gibbon allegedly said of the Athenians that people have continually been willing to sacrifice their political freedom to thwart real or perceived threats to their personal, group, or collective security: "In the end, more than they wanted freedom, they wanted security. They wanted a comfortable life and they lost it all — security, comfort, and freedom. When the Athenians [or Americans?] finally wanted not to give to society, but for society to give to them, when the freedom they wished for most was freedom from responsibility, then Athens ceased to be free."[15]

The U.S. historian Eric Foner shows clearly in his book *The Story of American Freedom,* the notion of "freedom" has different meanings. In fact, he shows that certain ways of thinking about freedom that are widespread among many on the political "right" are alien to the ideas of freedom in most of the world's other developed democracies. This is expressed in "negative liberty": absolute freedom from government control not only in such areas as land and gun ownership but also laissez-faire forms of economics as well (often called "economic freedom"[16]). On the other hand "positive liberty" involves a responsibility to exercise our freedom in accordance with certain fundamental moral laws rather than the laws of the "free" market. This is more a "freedom *for*" than a "freedom *from.*" Freedom *for* grounds one's own freedom in such attitudes as respect and concern for others based on their universal dignity as children of God. It brings together the rights involved with "to be" as well as the responsibility "to be with" in ways that promote the common good.

In a moving description integrating both forms of freedom, Jean Vanier writes: "To be free is to put justice, truth, and service to others over and above our own personal gain or our need for recognition, power, honor, and success. This freedom does not seek personal honors; it believes all, hopes all, bears all, and endures all. Freedom does not judge or condemn but understands and forgives. Freedom is liberation from all those inner fears that make us hide from people and from reality."[17]

In moving from freedom to trust as constituents of care, we find trust as that dynamic that gets built into a relationship where people are free from fear and intimidation along with being autonomous and self-individuated. The resulting security that comes from trusting relationships is the antidote to fear and intimidating ways. When trust defines a relationship, the power dynamics involved are exercised in a way that one's influence vis-à-vis the other in the relationship is credible, trustworthy, and honest. Trusting on the part of one and trustworthiness or loyalty on the part of the other balances a relationship of trust between two different entities. In an eroding relationship among people affected by the abuse of power on the part of some, trust is always one of the first casualties. Trust is another word for credibility on the part of all those influenced by a relationship. Given that the 2007 General Social Survey of the United States showed that the percentage of people who believe that, generally speaking, people can be trusted was at an all-time low in 2006[18] does not bode well for our belief in each other to create among ourselves a "community" or "culture of care."

In his book on church ministry, the Lutheran pastor Michael W. Foss writes of the church what can be said of every grouping of significance: "Money is not the currency that funds the church. Trust is. No matter how big or small the church, when trust is broken, conflict and separation occur. When trust is present, the people grow, the church grows, and the work of God gets done."[19] Trust is the necessary prerequisite for every healthy relationship, be it communal or collective, familial or institutional. When trust is broken it can be restored, but only when care is strengthened to the point where those who have been hurt can risk again.

Some time ago I had been asked by a community of women religious to give them a day of input. Those planning the day had booked me to come but asked me to be open to a topic that they thought would evolve, the more they interacted with the nuns. Finally they settled on a topic that would address a problem they had discovered: distrust among them was eroding their bonds. They asked me to speak on the dynamics of distrust and trust, telling me that the individualism that only in the last generation had become the hallmark of the sisters was destroying the possibility of trust among them. As a result their power had become overpowering rather than empowering. The more we go "our own way," the less possible will be the creation of a community of affirmation and challenge in which the members will grow in genuine freedom and degrees of trust, even in those who believe they are somehow grounded in a religious covenant or bonding.

When we met, two charts had been put on a wall, each with a large circle and a smaller inner circle saying "Trust" on one chart and "Distrust" on the other. In the outer circle were the words "God," "Self," "Others." In the "Distrust" circle the participants wrote a host of words and feelings that came to mind regarding each kind of relationship: angry, frustrated, isolated, devastated, anxious, disempowered, sad, outsider, hurt, shamed, alone, defensive, diminished, withdrawn, incapable, not understood, fear, inhibited, pained, passive-aggressive, humiliated, alone. In contrast, the synonyms and emotions articulated on the "Trust" circle represented positive dynamics: empowerment, joyful, wholeness, energized, whole, radiant, affirmed, growing, self-possessed, loved, warm, responsible, birthed, accepted, integrated, safe, belonging, respected, free, one, reliant.

A "holding environment" grounded in dynamics of mutual affirmation and confirmation, correction and challenge, will enkindle the fires of freedom and the treasure of trust among its members. Such a trusting environment will be characterized by true authenticity because the members will feel safe and free to say what may be in their hearts about the past, present, or future. This authenticity will enable and empower them to be increasingly transparent with each other. The greater the transparency, the more trust is engendered. The more authenticity and transparency characterize the community dynamics, the more the members will want to remain committed to each other. Building on the groundbreaking insights of Donald Winnicott regarding "holding environments," Robert Kegan describes them as involving a triad of confirmation, contradiction, and continuity (i.e., commitment for the long haul). Kegan's "confirmation" involves the affirmation of "holding on," his "contradiction" contains the dynamic of challenge, correction, and change, or "letting go," and "continuity" indicates the concomitant "sticking around" that characterizes all committed relationships.[20]

When trust defines relationships among those who care I can be myself without being judged defective, even as I may be challenged about my thinking, emotions, and actions. I can share my true opinions and feelings and they will be honored, although not always affirmed. When trust defines our relationships integrity results: those involved can rely on each other's words and promises. Trust frees us from the fear of being abused and being hurt; it empowers us to confide in others and they in us, without our "confidences" (i.e., our "entrustments") being violated.

When trust trumps distrust healthy relationships can result. Even when distrust has occurred because of abuse and other dynamics on the top part of the Power Chart, if healing begins, one can be more open to risk, taking the steps toward restored relationships. Unless the basic power dynamics in unequal power arrangements are transformed, there will be dysfunctional relationships.

The Connection between Care and Justice

At the core of the Great Command to "love our neighbor as ourselves" as well as the Golden Rule about "doing unto others as you would have them do unto you" is the assumption of basic equality. This assumes that a kind of mutuality exists among the parties in such a relationship — be that relationship communal or collective, familial or institutional. Indeed, care for others and their right to have their basic needs realized undergirds the very global reality. This has been enshrined in the Universal Declaration of Human Rights. This notion of the connection between care and justice (i.e., "right relationships among people and their resources") constitutes the core of communities of care themselves.

In her book *Starting at Home: Caring and Social Policy,* Nel Noddings brings these thoughts together when she states:

> The key, central to care theory, is this: caring-about (or, perhaps, a sense of justice) must be seen as instrumental in establishing the conditions under which caring-for can flourish. Although the preferred form of caring is caring-for, caring-about can help in establishing, maintaining and enhancing it. Those who care about others in the justice sense must keep in mind that the objective is to ensure that caring actually occurs. Caring-about is empty if it does not culminate in caring relationships.[21]

In my other writings, I have analyzed the levels of the world using the metaphor of home or *house* from the Greek word *oikía*. I have found that the "house" that needs to be rightly ordered in our own lives is found in the integration of our public image and our private *selves*. Our group relations based on justice for each person vis-à-vis the right sharing of resources constitutes the *oikonomía;* the *oikoumene* represents the inhabited world of our economic, political, and religious lives, while the *oikología* is a made-up word denoting the need for the first three forms of the *oikía* to be so ordered that the universe itself will be "right" or just.

When the underlying structures in the institutions of the *oikoumene* are unequal, we have seen, those institutions will be organized around various "isms" or unequal power relationships. Furthermore, they will protect themselves with an ideology that justifies those uncaring and unjust relationships by declaring they are "rightly ordered" or the only way such relationships can be structured. When this ideology is religiously reinforced with appeals to God, the ideology is protected by a theology that actually denigrates God and, therefore, becomes idolatrous. The only way to liberation from such ideology is non-participation in its lies, at least in our minds if it can't happen in our actual lives and professions.

While "faith" represents what is ultimate in the narratives as found in our culture's and church's "stories," oftentimes those narratives are defined by ideologies that compromise the ideal because of what Robert Schreiter calls "the narrative of the lie." He notes that, while "we humans cannot survive without a narrative of identity," when a few get control of the group narrative to serve their own self-interests rather than the good of the people's, their narratives are not considered, if not actually discounted. The result of this "narrative of the lie" is a kind of violence that "tries to destroy the narratives that sustain people's identities" in a way that every oppressor seeks to "substitute narratives of its own."[22] When the controlling group's self-serving narrative becomes the official ideology, all are expected to believe in it as a matter of faith, as the way to redemption and salvation.

Schreiter developed his notion of the "narrative of the lie" precisely to address the desired ideal of reconciliation among peoples once defined by the structured ordering of relationships called "apartheid" in South Africa. Reconciliation in such a place, he argued, must be grounded in truth-telling about the reality rather than an ideology of the lie that obfuscates and, therefore, perpetuates the unhealthy consequences of that sinful situation. Reconciliation is impossible among people who are forced to endure unequal power relationships.

Given the opening subheading of this chapter, "Who/What Can Care?" we turn to the next chapter, which begins by asking whether or not care-as-justice can be realized at the level of the *oikoumene,* especially when its structured relationships are defined by unequal power dynamics that, constitutively, make such ordering unjust by definition.

Chapter Eleven

Signs of Healthy Relationships

Addressing the Main Obstacles to a Healthy Society

History has almost always been written by the victors. It has been the lot of the victims to endure reading that history and being told it is true.

It has only been during my lifetime that significant books were written about U.S. history that told its story from the perspective of the Native Americans, who were overcome by outside forces successful by the power of their military prowess. Only when feminism became a significant voice in cultural and women's studies did women's experience and role in society become acknowledged as the force that it has been.

In the Roman Church, dominated by Western Europeans and their offspring, the same reality unfolded. It was not until 1971, I believe, that enough "others" became part of the leadership group that another perspective on "the world" could be articulated. This occurred when the 1971 Synod of Bishops was convened to discuss the topic "Justice in the World." For the first time in the Roman Church's history, a critical mass of the "victims" became large enough and, therefore, powerful enough to have its voice heard in a way that its experience would influence those traditionally immune to its cry. The sheer numbers of the bishops representing countries throughout the "developing world" forced the bishops of the former colonizing nations (be that colonization through politics, economics, or militarism) to listen. To use the image of Nel Noddings, the reality of uncare and injustice that was remote was made very "proximate" by their presence and witness. The result was a document that, for the first time (and only time that I can recall), acknowledged the structural injustice that included the church itself. Recalling the discussion in the previous chapter about how care must be grounded in the dignity of persons and the need for all persons to have access to their basic needs, the first three paragraphs of their document, *Justice in the World*, state the purpose of their gathering, the reality of global injustice and the recognition that they themselves needed to be converted if "the divine plan for the salvation of the world" would be realized. Thus the opening lines in the introduction state:

1. Gathered from the whole world, in communion with all who believe in Christ and with the entire human family, and opening our hearts to the Spirit who is making the whole of creation new, we have questioned ourselves about the mission of the People of God to further justice in the world.

2. Scrutinizing the "signs of the times" and seeking to detect the meaning of emerging history, while at the same time sharing the aspirations and questionings of all those who want to build a more human world, we have listened to the Word of God that we might be converted to the fulfilling of the divine plan for the salvation of the world.

3. Even though it is not for us to elaborate a very profound analysis of the situation of the world, we have nevertheless been able to perceive the serious injustices which are building around the world of men a network of domination, oppression and abuses which stifle freedom and which keep the greater part of humanity from sharing in the building up and enjoyment of a more just and fraternal [i.e., "caring"] world.[1]

The last paragraph seems like a social analysis of the way the dynamics in the top part of our Power Chart get structured in our world via a "network" or system of domination, oppression, and abuses that are ordered in such a way that these relationships undermine the very possibility of a truly free, trusting, and caring world.

The first step in conversion is non-participation and non-promotion of "the lie" that teaches the delusional belief that the existing order of sin is grace. Thus the bishops recognized the "sin of the world" represented by social injustice demanded their conversion. They also had the grace to make an "examination of conscience" and admit that this social sin — which demands conversion — might also exist in the structures and style of life within the church itself. Thus, as a universal body of bishops, they wrote one of the most potentially critical statements about the possibility of injustice within the institutional church itself, which, unfortunately, has never been addressed again as demanding conversion by any universal gathering of bishops.[2] Again the document offers an opening to address a way of ecclesiastical conversion which, unfortunately and despite ever more public witnesses of the need for it, has never been seriously structured:

40. While the Church is bound to give witness to justice, she recognizes that anyone who ventures to speak to people about justice must first be just in their eyes. Hence we must undertake an examination of the modes of acting, and of the possessions and life style found within the Church herself.

41. Within the Church rights must be preserved. No one should be deprived of his ordinary rights because he is associated with the Church in one way or another....

42. We urge that women should have their own share of responsibility and participation in the community life of society and likewise of the Church.

43. We propose that this matter be subjected to a serious study employing adequate means: for instance a mixed commission of men and women, religious and lay people, of differing situations and competence.

44. The Church recognizes everyone's right to suitable freedom of expression and thought. This includes the right of everyone to be heard in a spirit of dialogue which preserves a legitimate diversity within the Church.[3]

The Connection between Healthy Individuals and Groups and Their Wider World

Healthy relationships depend on healthy individuals. In our families and workplaces as well as in our institutions our relationships will be as healthy as the caring of the individuals that constitute them. The more unhealthy and uncaring dynamics we bring into our relationships, the more unstable they will be. The first step in becoming a healthy person is to become free of the negative, unhealthy forces that keep us from becoming healthy or to overcome those harmful, hurting dynamics that keep us from being healthy and helpful, including those "networks" or structures that serve as obstacles to becoming healthy. Once we are freed from the negative forces that keep us unhealthy, we will be free to become truly caring people, especially when we realize that harm done among us as people usually arises from a lack of care.[4]

Healthy individuals are those who have developed a certain self-image or identity that makes them think, feel, and act toward themselves (and others) in non-controlling ways. This creates a sense of security and safety in us, in our "I am." Consequently, the first step in feeling healthy is to be free of others' control, free of fear and intimidation, and free of those dangers and forms of abuse that define dynamics at the top level of our Power Chart. In other words, as any medical doctor will tell us, the main way of being healed involves the dynamics of "prevention."

A very common medical practice geared to prevention of disease is staying away from sick people; other forms of prevention involve immunization and inoculation. These practices must find their parallel practice in our relationships. At all levels of life we need to find ways to be free of those kinds of relationships that create dis-ease among us. We have to develop patterns of thinking, feeling, and acting that will inoculate us from falling into negative patterns lest they become destructive.

Control is the infectious disease of humanity that we have inherited as humans; we are continually told we must live in its debilitating and sickly environment, and we are always tempted to pass on this disease to others. Becoming a healthy "I am" means that we do not give to others the power to control how we think, feel, or act. To do so is to become co-dependent. Co-dependent persons are those whose own personal thinking, feeling, and acting are controlled by the thinking, feeling, and expectations of forces outside their individual "I am's." Co-dependents, by definition, are under the control of powers outside themselves. Becoming healthy, as I learned when I went into residential treatment to deal with my own issues of co-dependency, means learning not to give to others my power, my "I am." It means becoming free of making my thinking, feeling, and actions depend on theirs. It means never questioning the fundamental goodness that defines my "I am."

Becoming Self-Defined and Self-Directed

Some years ago I provided input to a large group of Roman Catholic women religious. This group of sisters had spent a year working together, along with their associates, on a directional statement for themselves and their corporate effort. In the midst of the wider Roman Catholic Church, with its clerical leaders making sure that their male-control will not be challenged, this group of women sculpted their directional statement around the opening declaration: "We are self-defined and self-directed." As it was read there was a kind of gasp among all in attendance and then a loud, liberating applause. This group chose to be healthy rather than co-dependent on the clergy.

On leaving that group en route to the airport to fly to another part of the United States to be with another, totally different group of women religious, I reflected on the contrast. I said to those in the car, who were still energized by what had been concluded by the weekend: "I am leaving a group of people who have chosen to stop being co-dependent and to be healthy. I am going to another group of women who won't even know what this means."

Part of the process of becoming free of the negative energy defined in dynamics of control around, among, and within us comes with such self-definition and self-direction. In my own individual life, I found that negativity was influencing me to such a degree that it was controlling me. Aware of the debilitating power and its affect on my psychological and social health, I decided I needed to enter treatment. As I did so, I discovered I needed to find ways to affirm myself, since I was not open to find such affirmation outside. This involved listening to others nurture me with "positive affirmations" in ways that I could appropriate in order to compensate for the negative critiques of others that I had internalized over many, many years. This means becoming free of the controlling and paralyzing force of such negative critiques. It means to stop listening to such voices in ways that will continue to debilitate me and only make me angrier inside (or outside).

When I become free of the negative voices that try to control me in destructive ways of thinking, feeling, and acting about my "I am" and when I develop a positive sense of myself, I can move to find my security in my "self" rather than others.

A healthy relationship with others builds on a positive attitude toward oneself. It also involves the ability to "stand up" for oneself in the midst of negative expressions of power. A "healthy" example of this, I think, is the story of a father and son riding a crowded subway train in New York that I read about in the *New York Times* "Metropolitan Diary," which is always part of my breakfast on Monday mornings. The writer recalled:

> I was riding a very crowded No. 7 train on a very hot Friday after-noon with the goal of catching the L.I.R.R.'s 4:06 Cannonball to the Hamptons.
>
> As the train approached Hunters Point, I overheard the man behind me giving directions to his young son, approximately eight years old:
>
> "O.K., as soon as the doors open, start pushing and shoving."[5]

Healthy Relationships as Energized by Care

While "pushing and shoving" may be acceptable survival dynamics in urban life, they become destructive when they get translated into our day-to-day life and work. When the latter arrangements are grounded in affirmation and care, which are continually progressing in the ability to be free with each other in ways that engender mutual trust, health in the relationship will be the result. Any pushing and shoving will have given way to trusting and loving. This does not mean that there won't be times that a healthy relationship won't have pain or hurt. But it does mean the core relationship will be constructive of right relationships — whether these be between spouses, with families, or between nations in the family of nations.

When I was a child, we lived by certain family ground rules. To disobey them invited sanctions. If my father or mother considered the violation severe enough, we would be spanked. However, when we were being spanked the hurt incurred was somehow offset by the words all children in such "environments of care" hear in such situations: "This hurts me more than it hurts you."

What does this mean? Having pondered why my mother would say this as she beat our rears with the razor strap, I think it involves two things: first, she was deeply saddened that the relationship of trust had been broken, and, second, she was hurt that she felt she had no other recourse than this form of discipline. Today's child psychologists might disagree with the physical way she chose to implement the sanctions, but not the sentiment of care that characterized the discipline. I do not believe she abused her power; in fact, I believe it confirmed her as a powerful caring person who had only my health as a person at stake.

What does it mean to be a healthy person, to have a healthy marriage, or to be healthy in terms of the various social indexes that measure a nation or institution's "well-being"? At its core, I believe it is the sense of security that comes from belonging to a community of care in which people are free and trust prevails.

A former colleague of mine, Fred Cavaiani, is now a psychologist. He insists that "consistent caring is the basis of a healthy life." He came to this realization over time, but it was crystallized when he twisted an ankle and immediately had caregivers around him trying to help him in his injury. He reflected:

> Children who are raised with consistent caring shown by caring words but backed up by caring actions grow up to be healthy and successful. People are healed by caregivers who show their care in loving words but are backed up by consistent and loving actions. Physicians, nurses, lawyers, psychologists, marriage counselors, hospice workers, teachers, and many more change the world

into a better place by their consistent caring for people. These are people who show care not just by kind words but also by prompt service, returning phone calls, and a high degree of respect for the other person shown by caring actions. We notice and remember people who show us love and respect.[6]

Being a healthy person means doing what one can to right the wrongs we have done as well as the wrongs done to others in society, no matter how far away they may be. In this sense I realized, as a Milwaukeean, that I could bring positive energy to a situation of violence in New York City. Following the example of one of my confreres, who makes a point of visiting the place where in our city someone has been killed and praying for an alternative way of settling disputes, I read with interest the story of the murder of Pravin Shah, a newsstand operator at West Thirty-Fourth Street and Eighth Avenue in Manhattan in 1994. A few days after his killing, I found myself exiting the subway precisely at the point where he had been gunned down. I took a few minutes and sent the healing energy that was in me to try to bring about another force for good where it had been taken away so recently.

Healthy Relationships with Self and Others Creating Wellness

The goal of life for every person is to become integrated. The goal of communal life is health among its members. The dream of society is rightly ordered relationships that will prevent the outbreak of war. Another word for these goals is "wellness" at the personal, group, and collective levels of life. The process of achieving this wellness begins with each individual. In this sense, wellness is the goal of life, not just health.

People can be racked with pain from a sickness, but they can be well. Disease may have invaded what seems like every part of one's body, but a sense of wellness will exude from their spirit. I found this in the reaction of my brother, Pat, when the doctor came to tell him that he had four weeks to three months to live. He said: "I'm not going to ask why this is happening to me; I'm not going to get angry. I've lived a good life." In other words, his body was dying but his "I am" was solidly well.

In his book *Wellness,* John Pilch distinguishes wellness from health:

> To begin with, health is something you can do for yourself, as well as something someone else can do for you. A surgeon can

return your ailing heart muscle to health by performing bypass surgery. Wellness, on the other hand, is entirely self-created and self-directed. "You alone do it, but you don't do it alone." There is no wellness practitioner but you, the individual person.[7]

If health is wellness in any body (i.e., our physical bodies, our groups, the body-public, or any other organization), we can ask: What constitutes any body that is well? Why do some people develop self-defeating behaviors such as negative anger, depression, and addiction? As he observed others in the Nazi concentration camps, Victor Frankl discovered that people could be in totally negative surroundings but were able not only to survive but also to have an inner strength to the degree that they found meaning in their lives. In this meaning they found direction for their lives. Part of this sense of meaning came from their decision not to participate in the controlling actions of their guards and the Nazis. They chose to live lives of meaning and purpose. This led them to choose to care in the midst of a climate of control. When people stopped having a purpose in their lives they lost their desire to live.

Recently, a great surprise at the *New York Times* came with the realization that the best-selling book in the United States was Rick Warren's *The Purpose-Driven Life*. Throughout the nation groups were formed of people committed to take forty days to read its message and act on it. Many found great meaning and healing in reading the book and sharing its contents.

I tried reading the book, but something in me resisted. After wondering if there was something wrong with me, since so many others were finding the book and sessions to be so beneficial and healing, I came to realize that I had already embraced a "purpose-driven life." By so doing, I had found meaning and fidelity to that "higher purpose" in life many of us call "God." I had come to understand that God had a goal not only for me but also for all who would listen. It can be summarized in one sentence from the prophet Micah. After examining those required behaviors defined by the Law as it had been interpreted through the ages by those in power (often to satisfy their other-than-divine purposes), the statement is made: "You have been told what is good [i.e., for your good or wellness] and what it is that is required of you: to do justice, to love tenderly, and to walk humbly with God" (Micah 6:8).

When I break down the triad outlined by Micah, justice involves my need to be in right-relationships with everyone and to work for right-relationships at every level of my world; loving tenderly means to live in care in ways that will bring positive energy to everyone and everything;

and walking humbly with God means always acknowledging the fact that there is a Higher Power beyond my own and trying to remain in that Power by never trying to overpower or de-energize any others. When I live from this triad, I have found meaning and purpose in my life. I have also accepted my part in empowering others to live a "purpose-driven" life.

Chapter Twelve

Constructing Relationships
That Channel Anger in Positive Ways

One of the main reasons we remain in negative, debilitating anger is our denial of its force in our hearts, in our thinking, feeling, and acting. One of the easiest ways this gets expressed is when one says loudly or with gritted teeth: "I am not angry!" Rather than "stuff anger," we do better psychologically when we name it, claim it, and tame it toward constructive purposes. Otherwise it will "eat us up." Naming the anger involves an admission of its power at work in our hearts and determining what negative forms of power or lack of positive forms of power resulted in its abiding in our hearts. Claiming the anger involves an admission of its force in our thinking and feeling. Taming it involves directing it into dynamics of care rather than control.

A key way we can remain in our own anger (and, therefore, in control of others through it) is to accuse *them* of "just being angry." Another way those in control can threaten any who challenge is to ask: "What is your problem?" At the level of those who want to maintain systems of abuse, you get men accusing feminists as being "radical" or "angry" or just plain "wanting power" (which really means they want "my male group's control"). Carolyn Osiek writes:

> If there is any one negative image that is most frequently attached to feminism by those who fear it, it is that of "those angry women." Anger in women seems to jar loose a great deal of primitive and irrational terror from both men and women who observe it. For Freudians, it evokes fear of rejection and separation from the Mother. Jungians see it as the embodiment of the violent and vindictive Anima. The receptive, nurturing aspect of the feminine, so desperately needed in a violent world, seems to have been abandoned to the destructive forces of human darkness. When women do not stabilize society, society is not stabilized.[1]

Anger threatens those whose own control depends on maintaining such debilitating "stability." Indeed, victims of structural injustice, when awareness comes, will be angry; they will be "justifiably angry."

Before I entered residential treatment for my anger, I projected this problem onto others. Now that I have recognized my negative anger, I have found it necessary to relate to others in a way free of the negative dynamics of anger. Now, I find people who attend my workshops saying things like: "Mike, fifteen years ago I listened to you, but it was very hard because you were so angry. Now I feel the same passion and conviction, but it doesn't frighten me; I don't find myself needing to protect myself." Other say things like: "You are as committed to your beliefs as ever, but I don't feel the 'edge of anger' in what you say or how you say it." In other words, it seems, they are finding my anger moving from resentment and rage to passion and zeal. Or, at least, I certainly hope this may be so!

In Greek, a thin line exists between the words for passion and persecution. In other words, my passion can result in your persecution. For instance, in my more controlling days, I felt I'd be less than honest if I did not "tell it like it is." And I let the chips fall where they may. I was uncaring about how the one receiving or experiencing my "truth" was affected. Now I still want to "tell it like it is" by being faithful to the truth, but there is something more involved than simply being faithful to telling the truth to another. It involves the way we do the truth-telling.

Once we know our anger is undermining our relationships, we can choose to be defined by it or to begin to overcome its negative expressions. Then our anger can become constructive. When this happens, I can be angry in ways that promote the good rather than feed into the negative. Authentic and healthy anger does not de-energize others and ourselves. On the contrary, it becomes energizing, a force for good, a source of mobilizing energies to bring about the good. It engages us fully in creative thinking, positive feeling, and constructive action.

The Practice of Mindfulness

Mindfulness is the way we become consciously connected in ever widening circles of care throughout the created order. It is a discipline that is learned and developed only through constant practice.

While I was taught in the seminary to practice awareness of the "presence of God" in all things, I have found even more benefit in the practice of mindfulness from my readings in Buddhism.

Buddhism is built on the premise that all suffering in the world arises from attachment to material and transient things, including ideas and perceptions to which we often cling. We have already seen that such disordered desires create conflicts in, among, and around us. However, by the process of dispassion, we gradually become free of those disordered desires. When we no longer give power to or feed their cravings, we eventually free ourselves of our irrational desires with regard to material and transient matters. While Buddhism embraces the "eightfold path" as the way to overcome attachment-induced suffering, I have found a very helpful path in doing the practice of mindfulness.

Mindfulness is a form of meditation. In it we pay direct attention to the "now," to the power of each moment. It is a way of releasing the healing energy we all have within us. It is the practice of potentially unlocking this power by cultivating the healing potential of our minds by focusing them on bringing good to whoever and whatever may enter our minds that we may be more consciously connected to them. Thich Nhat Hanh writes in his *Living Buddha, Living Christ* that "mindfulness is very much like the Holy Spirit. Both are agents of healing." He adds:

> In Buddhism, our effort is to practice mindfulness in each moment — to know what is going on within and all around us. When the Buddha was asked, "Sir, what do you and your monks practice?" he replied, "We sit, we walk, and we eat." The questioner continued, "But sir, everyone sits, walks, and eats," and the Buddha told him, "When we sit, we *know* we are sitting. When we walk, we *know* we are walking. When we eat, we *know* we are eating." Most of the time, we are lost in the past or carried away by future projects and concerns. When we are mindful, touching deeply the present moment, we can see and listen deeply, and the fruits are always understanding, acceptance, love, and the desire to relieve suffering and bring joy.[2]

In my own life mindfulness offers me a way of slowing down and connecting with myself in a way that puts my surface-self at the service of my real-self. This happens when I recall my mantra that ends with a desire that I spend my life by caring, by "being kind."

> May I be safe from inner and outer dangers.
> May I be sound and peaceful in mind.
> May I be strong in soul and body.
> May I spend my life by being kind.

Mindfulness also finds us consciously as well as potentially connected to everyone in the universe. I find myself practicing mindfulness at various times throughout the day: while shopping at the store and considering the realities of those in the aisles with me; watching others who are inconvenienced by flight delays; or even swimming in my lane when some others might get upset because I may have entered "their space." I find myself repeating the mantra over and over, this time, thinking of them (or whoever else may come to mind, including those with whom I may strongly disagree in terms of their politics, economics, or ecclesiology):

> May he/she/they be safe from inner and outer danger.
> May he/she/they be sound and peaceful in mind.
> May he/she/they be strong in soul and body.
> May he/she/they/ spend his/her/their life/lives by being kind.

As a Franciscan I have been inspired by my founder, Francis of Assisi, to be consciously connected with everything in creation itself because all these "things" are my mother, my brother, and my sister. Thus, when I think of other forms of creation I also can be mindful (especially in this age of global warming which makes us aware of our deep, ecological connectedness) of everything on earth as I reflect:

> May he/she/it/they be safe from inner and outer danger.
> May he/she/it/they be sound and peaceful in mind.
> May he/she/it/they be strong in soul and body.
> May he/she/it/they spend his/her/their life/lives by being kind.

The Practice of Patience

Mindfulness is the parent of patience. The more I practice mindfulness, I have discovered, the more patient I become.

While working on this book I happened to be sitting on a plane with a thirtyish Arab American. She was a financial consultant for a large Wall Street firm. She held dual citizenship but would not return to her country of origin for fear that her father, who resided there, would take her under his control and not allow her to leave. In the midst of our conversation and my sharing with her the various dimensions of the Power Chart, which she found very applicable in her life as an individual, in her relationships, and in her unique dual nationality, she stopped at the word "anger" on the chart. "You know what?" she asked me, "Patience is the antidote of anger. Whenever I find myself getting angry, I stop and take a deep breath and try to be patient. I am amazed at the peace that comes to me."

One of the Greek words for anger is *thymós,* being short-tempered. Our English language has translated that Greek into anger images such as "short fused." When we choose to use our anger as a constructive power, our *thymós* turns into *macrothymía:* patience. While everything around us seems geared to "hurrying up" and "quicker," patience invites us to approach delays and slowdowns and traffic jams from another perspective. Patience refuses to give power to forces beyond us. Patience involves the way we use our power when we don't want to direct our anger in negative ways. According to M. J. Ryan in her book *The Power of Patience,* "It's about holding back when you want to let loose, putting up with something you'd rather not and waiting for something to happen rather than forcing it along." She notes that not all things "can be accomplished through will power. Sometimes what we need is a bit of wait power." Convinced that patience is the glue that holds society together, the essence of "diplomacy and civility, lawfulness and civil order," she concludes: "Without it, people can't work together and society can't function at all."[3]

Patience is one of the hardest virtues for me to cultivate. Ever since I would ask, "Are we there yet," when we took a trip, I think my impatience stems from the fact that I am an intense and idealistic person. (It goes without saying that I am also a person who has liked to be in control!). It might also be because I am a man and, as such, women will tell us, patience is not found among us too easily, if at all. As the saying goes: "Patience is a virtue. Try it if you can. Seldom found in women. Never found in man."

The Practice of Passion

Passion represents the direction of our energy toward the realization of the good. Sometimes it results as a reaction to right what is wrong in the world of individuals, groups, and structures. Other times it just represents deeply held convictions, emotions of solidarity, combined with a burning desire to bring about a greater good.

At the individual level of life, passion can be found in children who get very upset when things are "not fair." They have an inherent sense of right and wrong and feel anger when the wrong triumphs over what they believe to be right. In groups, a passion for right relationships empowers people toward reconciliation in the form of repentance and forgiveness. When we deal with the way power is unequal among various groupings of people that create the "isms" around dynamics of sex, race, age, orientation, nationality, ethnicity, geography, monetary worth, or pedigree, it is represented in an obsession to make things right for everyone, especially the victims of the unequal power relationships. This is called the passion for justice.

For many, their initial efforts to work for social justice, or to right structural inequities, arise from their awareness of the disparities that benefit one group at the expense of another or the whole. This results in a sense of anger — but this kind of anger arises from the power of care. The anger experienced gets directed positively in a passionate commitment to bring about change. As our Power Chart illustrates, this passionate commitment to bring about change and to right wrongs itself has a negative way of getting expressed as well as a positive way.

In my early days of working for social justice, I often wondered why so many people were afraid of me and intimidated by my intensity and commitment to whatever cause I may have promoted. After finding more and more people shying away from me or just plain avoiding me, I heard Three Dog Night sing a verse of the song "Easy to Be Hard." In one of the verses it said that many people working for social justice were "hard-hearted" — passionate about social justice issues and the "bleeding crowd," but unfeeling in one-to-one relationships. I found myself being convicted by that statement in the song.

Miriam Ukeritis has articulated how these ways of thinking and feeling can be self-destructive as well as cause-destructive. In commenting on the passionate attitude that conveys the message "Do it my way or forget it," she writes that such a way of thinking comes out of an attitude akin to "if I'm doing, everybody should."

> That means that if I am "into" the charismatic renewal, you have to find Jesus the way I have found him. If I am involved in pro-life politics no one who is outside my single issue campaign is interested in life. Feminists coming from such a stance tell us that we cannot know our oppression as women until we totally reject all men.[4]

Ukeritis describes such thinking as an "either/or" perspective, which is intolerant of differences as well as other people's freedom to think, feel, and come to behavioral decisions that may be alternative to our own. Basically, she says it represents "a very primitive level of anger, and does not revere the other person."[5] In other words, it is based on control rather than care.

When our care for "the least" among us drives us not only to meet their immediate needs directly but also to work to change those social relationships that create their unmet needs in the first place or do nothing to alleviate them in the second place, our passion for justice is on the right track. However, when we become passionate about any social injustice that results in various "isms" and systemic violence, we will easily be called "angry people" by those whose interests (i.e., "control") is being challenged.

Why, in the face of one form of inequity and unfairness and one manifestation of social injustice and violence, do we resist allowing our innate sense of anger to make us passionate promoters of change — be it individual, group, or social? I think much of it revolves around dynamics operable at the top level of our Power Chart. Because the manipulation and exploitation, the domination and coercive forms of control have become so institutionalized and, therefore, legitimized, we fear being rejected. Hence we develop a kind of lukewarmness in the face of the victims and victimization occurring around us. We fall into indifference.

Fear and intimidation can be powerful blockages to any passion for right relationships that would be about a greater equality among persons, groups, and entities within our structures especially related to power dynamics and the "isms." So not only our fear of being rejected, but our fear of being isolated and abandoned, our fear of failure and of "stepping out" from the accepted norms, can become the effective forces that immunize and inoculate us from passion for that kind of fairness and justice that will bring about greater equality among disparate peoples and, as a result, greater and more equal power sharing among them all.

At this point, I find it fascinating that Ukeritis will go so far as to say that, if we don't get angry when faced with unequal power relationships, if we don't get incensed at injustice, we commit a "sin" ourselves. In other words, there is a "righteous anger" that should arise in us at the realization of so much injustice among and beyond us. If we don't get angry, she argues, we will be unrighteous or sinners. In images that can find their echoes in the words spelled out on our Power Chart she writes:

> Anger is a powerful, a potentially immensely creative passion. We can compare it to love whose opposite, in terms of energy, is not hate but apathy. If the opposite of anger is non-feeling, numbness, death, then anger might be considered a virtue. Thus, we could define anger as a habit of passionate devotion to all humanity's participation in the banquet of life, and staunch opposition to all that is death-dealing. In this case, anger is a virtue....

Not to be angry is a sin when my lack of passion condones a death-dealing situation. I cannot witness to complicity with a situation that is anti-life.[6]

The Practice of Zeal

When we consider the notion of "zeal," we find different thoughts about it, depending on whether we are on the giving or receiving ends of it. Zeal to one person is obnoxious fanaticism to another. Zeal is one's willingness to be given to a cause, to become a zealot. The deeper the conviction about the righteousness of the cause, the greater will be one's zeal in realizing the goals of the cause. In a life path of care our goal is to direct anger into constructive zeal.

Zeal in the promotion of justice or right relationships at all levels is wonderfully expressed in the reaction of the disciples in John's Gospel to the cleansing of the Temple: they recalled the passage: "Zeal for your house will consume me" (John 1:17). If others observe how our energy is directed to challenge unjust structures that alienate and marginate, such zeal will show we too are expressing our anger productively and justly.

Here's a poignant example of retaining zeal but aiming it in a completely opposite direction from the way it had previously been deployed:

In the 1970s, during the Khmer Rouge era in Cambodia, Kang Kek Ieu, better known by his revolutionary nickname, Duch, was the head of its secret police and the commandant of Tuoi Sleng prison, where great numbers of people were tortured and killed. In his zeal to overcome the enemies of the Khmer Rouge, he gave orders to torture this or that person "even if it kills him." In the margins of a list of seventeen children, he simple wrote: "Kill them all."

In the twenty years since the Khmer Rouge were ousted from power, he converted to Christianity and devoted himself to spreading the Gospel and to helping refugees who fled the brutality of his regime. In his own transformation he relates to the story of another zealot whose zeal made him a persecutor who then became zealous for another cause. "I think my biography is something like Paul's," he told a reporter from the United States. "I feel very sorry about the killing and the past," he said. "I wanted to be a good Communist. Now in the second half of my life, I want to serve God by doing God's work to help people."[7]

If we practice mindfulness and patience it will take us down the road to constructive practices of passion and zeal. There we will have the energy or power to be able to turn conflict off and collaboration on.

Chapter Thirteen

Moving from Conflicts to Collaboration

Because of my work in challenging some of the practices of large corporations through socially responsible shareholder actions, I often get interviewed. I have discovered that, invariably, conflict sells newspapers; it is the teaser for the evening news. It's almost as if we depend on conflict in order to begin our day reading the news. Recently, though, I had the wonderful experience of getting my morning coffee and being greeted with a front-page headline that proved that conflict is not the only source of news. It's also news — good news — when people *dissipate* conflicts.

Some background: My city of Milwaukee continually finds itself on lists of the most segregated urban settings in the United States. Much disparity and distrust exist, especially between whites and non-whites, urbanites and suburbanites. As I was writing this book a conflict arose involving Michael McGee, a Milwaukee alderman and one of the main leaders in the African American community. He was parked in the lot of a Blockbuster video store in surburban Wauwatosa. When clerks were closing the store, they called police to report a suspicious person. The police came and tensions rose. An altercation ensued.

Two days later a predominantly African American rally took place in front of the Wauwatosa police station protesting the action against McGee. There, to support the police, was Russell D. Stoeckler. When a McGee supporter got too close to him, Stoeckler shoved him. The man retaliated, hitting Stoeckler with a bullhorn. A brawl followed, which made the headlines of the next day's paper. If similar past incidents were any indication, conflictive rhetoric and the potential for violence would quickly escalate.

However, all was deflated when the next day's *Milwaukee Journal Sentinel* showed a picture of Stoeckler at the rally being taken into custody by a Wauwatosa policeman. The headline read: " 'I Made a Dumb Mistake': Tosa Man Gets an Earful from His Wife, Decides to Apologize for His Role in Fight at McGee Rally." The paper quoted Stoeckler as

126

saying his wife was "very upset" by his outburst and concluded: "We need to build bridges now, not tear them apart."[1]

How did Russell Stoeckler, who had been a key player in the conflict, keep it from moving further, into war? He apologized; he admitted he was wrong; he sought to change the dynamics. That it was his wife who compelled him to apologize is probably no coincidence. How do husbands and wives stay together through years and decades of inevitable conflicts? They learn how to apologize.

Democratic strategist James Carville, who is married to Republican strategist Mary Matalin, was asked what makes a good husband. He replied with his signature wit, "Capitulation. Retreat. The ability to engage in vigorous agreement with one's wife at all times. I am the Neville Chamberlain of husbands. You want Czechoslovakia? Take it. Austria? It's yours."[2] Though facetious, his words offer a strong grain of wisdom.

Collaboration: The Antidote of Competition

Possibly the key obstacle to collaboration is competitiveness among those who are supposed to be working together. I know this from experience. During my college days, it happened that I was in very close proximity to Dale Olen. Although he was a year younger than me, I found I was jealous of him: his good looks, his personality, and his acumen at sports. It gave me pleasure when he failed and when I prevailed at almost anything. My need to be recognized as more significant than him as well as my desire to succeed was a great motivating power in my life. Unable to compete with him (i.e., achieve power and reputation) at those levels, I found myself competing with him to be the first to publish a book.

Years after we both graduated, I found myself allied with Dale on an issue related to social change. With the Vietnam War raging and igniting upheavals throughout the nation from cities to campuses, along with others we became convinced our group had to be more committed to concerns related to social justice and peace. It led me to fly to Kansas City to meet him. I had come from Milwaukee and he from Lawrence, Kansas, where he was getting his degree in social psychology.

As I landed I remember thinking to myself: "I don't want to compete with him anymore; I don't want to try to outdo him. I just want to find a way we can work together to bring this goal to realization." As I entered the terminal and we gave each other a bear hug I had the feeling that everything that reflected the past ways I had competed with him was history.

The conflict I felt with Dale because of my competitiveness (really a way of seeking to dominate in our relationship) had evaporated. Indeed, we soon began partnering on a team, with him as the team leader. Never again arose the old feelings of competitiveness and desire to dominate.

This moving from conflict to collaboration represents the process described by Riane Eisler, wherein partnering rather than domination characterize the dynamics of healthy groups.[3] When we truly believe "two heads are better than one" we are headed toward effective collaboration. When we learn the same in our groups, society will be better.

Who has not heard of the two groups of competing boy scouts who, realizing an upstream dam was breaking, started working together. A more recent example came in southern India in December 2005 in the wake of the infamous tsunami. Immediately Hindus and Muslims put aside their differences and partnered on relief efforts. A *Wall Street Journal* reporter noted: "Refugees in Samiyarpettai's main Hindu temple weren't surprised that aid was coming from the nearby Islamic community. Standing in front of a stature of Durga, the Indian goddess of protection, someone said, 'We're all fishermen here. Religion comes second.' "[4]

Collaborate or Die

As we entered this century, the brokerage firm J. D. Edwards ran a series of ads on collaboration, featuring various people holding signs with different sayings about the virtue of collaboration. The most recognized was "Collaborate or Die." My favorite, however, featured a graying man in his forties holding a sign in the middle of a busy intersection of people. It read: "Collaborate and Thrive."

My work finds me connected to the same group of men in our religious order as earlier in my life, but who now face the choice of not collaborating and therefore dying, or collaborating, believing by so doing we can thrive. We have had a history of being able to staff our own institutions. However, with declining numbers and fewer recruits, we find ourselves in need of the help of others not belonging to our group. This has led us to address the issue of collaboration. In other words, it is not the value of collaboration that has motivated us, but the need for it. Now we realize we must move from the "need for it" to discussing its value, to desiring it and committing ourselves to make it a reality.

In the initial stages of our work toward collaboration, we had workshops on the subject that brought in the experts and studies of our feelings toward it. Not surprisingly, it became clear that the key obstacles to pursuing it revolved around issues related to our corporate identity and our issues related to power, especially "our" power to control our own institutions and what takes place in and through them.

For years we had functioned in such a way by ourselves that our corporate identity had become equated with certain externalities rather than values we had as a mission that others beyond us would willingly embrace. Consequently, our corporate identity became threatened as we realized we would have to function in different ways if we were to continue functioning at all. This demanded a reexamination of our true identity. It could no longer be defined by externalities but by the mission itself. This demanded a movement from control to shared responsibility to bring about the goals we envisioned.

As to power, we saw it as a kind of a pie with certain parts rather than a dynamic, as a quantity that was limited rather than a quality that could be the source of a new kind of energy. In other words, for us power was a matter of staying in charge of the process. We were afraid of losing our power in the form of power itself, our monies, and our reputation. We wanted to keep controlling, claiming, and climbing, by ourselves, rather than finding new ways to continue doing the good that we had done in the past, but from the energy of another model.

Addressing this fear at one of our gatherings, the speaker we had hired challenged us:

> The main fear expressed in your feedback is in terms of losing control. Someone else will do the deciding. Someone else will do the spending. Someone else will do the hiring, etc., etc., etc. My response to that is: "Does the eye help the ear, or hinder it? Does the ear hurt the eye, or help it? Are the ear or the eye less ear or eye when they operate together? Neither loses identity. But both enhance the body."[5]

The healthy community is a corporate body whose individual members are free of the need to control, who affirm and correct each other in care, and who are growing in mutual trust. Its members have found ways to work together; its leaders realize the power inherent in such collaboration. They know that the greater the collaboration, the more powerful the results. Whether we will relate competitively or collaboratively depends on how we direct our energies, our power. If we continue to relate competitively it will be because we (un)consciously believe we have ultimate authority in such matters; if we decide to work collaboratively it will be because we believe in the age-old adage: "two heads are better than one." We will be playing in a symphony rather than performing a solo.

While any of the components on the top of the Power Chart undermine the possibility of directing our energies toward effective collaboration, I found this truth verified in Loughlan Sofield and Carroll Juliano's classic work on collaboration. Among the attitudes they list as obstacles to effective collaboration we find competitiveness first, followed by parochialism, arrogance, and burnout. Among the behaviors they see as obstacles to collaboration we find expressions of anger such as hostility and a basic unwillingness to deal with conflict.[6]

Conflict Management or Conflict Resolution?

Noting that there is a difference between conflict management and conflict resolution, Sofield and Juliano write:

> Many people approach conflict with the desire to resolve it, remove it and reinstate harmony. To expect to achieve this goal in all circumstances is unrealistic. While conflict resolution is possible, conflict management is often more realistic. Managing conflict means being able to live and work together even though the source of conflict has not been eliminated.[7]

I will admit that Sofield and Juliano have had a much greater involvement in addressing the topic of conflict than I have. However, I believe from my own personal experience as well as my work with conflicted groups that, unless we begin from the assumption that we should try to resolve conflicts rather than merely manage them, we can be headed toward further dysfunctionality in a group and more burnout and depression among the members of such groups.

In my mind, when we resort to functioning from a perspective of only being able to "manage" a conflict rather than "resolve" the dynamics that have created it, we have thrown in the towel. The basic reason why individuals and groups end up relating to each other in such ways is that they have lost trust in themselves or each other to seriously find alternative ways of relating.

When conflict management becomes the style of relating among people, it may define a way of coping with negativity in the hope that "they will grow out of it," such as parents hope will happen with teenagers. However, when conflicts are so great among groups that the only way to keep their members from further violence comes when it is decided "to send in the troops," it is truly a sad commentary on people's intransigency. So, instead of working to resolve conflicts in our inner cities, we send in more police, and when ethnic groups and different tribal groups are unwilling to go through conflict resolution, and the United Nations sends in more troops, nobody can be happy.

The Steps to Conflict Resolution

What happens when the dynamics that led to a conflict or may be sustaining a conflict have occurred for so long or have been expressed in dynamics that have been so debilitating that any collaboration seems doomed? I have found this never need be "the way it has to be." There are ways to resolve conflicts among us. However, just as it took steps to get into the conflict, it will take steps to resolve any conflict. In my experience, there are five steps that must be taken between conflicted parties if their differences are to be resolved.

Step One: Wanting a change. At least one in the conflict must want *it* to change; usually I want the other to change, thinking there's no reason for me to change. This desire often gets articulated in such statements as: "I don't want to keep fighting like this," or "Why can't we get beyond this." When at least one indicates a desire to address the issues, the other(s) involved, at a minimum, must be willing to go through the subsequent process. If not, the level of conflict will remain. The best you can do to keep it from moving to a break will be to manage it. However this will take its toll and there will be burnout of some sort.

Step Two: Engaging in active listening. Active listening is critical since most of us respond to challenges by defending why we were right in whatever led to the conflict. So we don't really listen to the others' concerns. However, with active listening, each person involved listens without interruption to the others' point of view on what led to and defines the conflict and then repeats back what has been heard. In the process we begin to see things from the other's perspective.

This happened to me when I was in conflict with a woman regarding our relationship itself. The conflict remained unresolved because we were defined by the dynamics that made it so: (1) we had unresolved tensions around the relationship, (2) these were based on unrealized expectations related to differing behaviors sought, and (3) these unrealized expectations arose from unagreed-upon assumptions related to the dynamics of the relationships itself.

Unable to resolve our conflicts, we came to a "break" in the relationship, as our Power Chart shows will happen. So we parted, unresolved in our conflicted relationship. Some years later we happened to be attending the same meeting, because of our work. When we greeted each other I asked her if she'd like to have dinner. She immediately agreed. However, as we went to the restaurant, I said: "I'm going around the country giving talks on conflict resolution. And you and I are conflicted. Would you like to see if we could do something to resolve it?" Again, she immediately agreed.

I explained to her that we had made the first step in resolving conflicts and that the second involved "active listening." So I agreed to listen to her interpretation of what happened in our relationship that made it conflicted. I told her I would not interrupt except to clarify what she was saying. So she started. And I had previously "heard" it all.

But then something happened. I started really listening — to her, not myself and my own defenses. I came to realize how things that I had done had really hurt her. At that I realized that I, by definition, had been abusive toward her insofar as abuse is "any way one uses to control another through fear and intimidation." I started to cry. However, since the "crying" part speaks to the fifth stage of resolving a conflict, let me move to the third and following steps.

Step Three: Truly understanding what we've heard. It follows that, since most misunderstanding arises from poor listening, once we truly listen to the other, we will begin to understand. We "stand under" the other, open to his or her interpretation, we move into the reality of the other. We decenter ourselves and become focused on the thinking, the feelings, and the past actions that have affected the other.

Step Four: Coming to a place of acceptance. This does not mean we accept the thinking and behaviors that may have been wrong; what we "accept" is the one who did the wrong. We distinguish between the one(s) who did the wrong and the wrong itself. While the wrong may be something that can never be accepted (such as abuse in its various forms), the one who did the wrong is understood in a way where acceptance can follow more easily.

Step Five: Admitting our own part in the conflict. Given our involvement in the previous four steps, we sincerely acknowledge how we ourselves contributed to the conflict. If the steps have been mutually shared, it should also follow that the others themselves will admit what they did that also influenced the conflict.

Ideally there are two more steps that should be taken to bring about a full restoration of a broken relationship. If the fifth step in conflict resolution finds me admitting the "exact nature of my wrong" that led to the conflict, this should lead invariably to the step Russell Stroecker took in the story that began this chapter: we apologize for our part in the conflict. If this is perceived to be sincere, with a firm purpose to avoid such behaviors in the future, it should elicit a seventh step on the part of the other: forgiveness.

When repentance and forgiveness take place in a conflicted relationship, reconciliation brings about a new way that brings all parties back to an equal footing. They can begin anew. They can begin working together rather than continue to tear each other apart. These are not the only reasons why reconciliation is important to work toward; in so doing, those involved are less prone to returning to the ways that led to the conflict in the first place. They are ready to collaborate, realizing with Sofield and Juliano that "it is not the presence of conflict which impedes the growth toward collaboration, but the lack of forgiveness and reconciliation."[8]

The Steps to Collaboration

In a November 7, 2005, lead article on "Managing" in the *Wall Street Journal,* the author began by declaring: "It turns out your high-school coach was right: Teamwork matters." He continues: "Research from a variety of settings, from hospital operating rooms to Wall Street, suggests that the way people work together is important for an endeavor's success — even in fields thought of as dominated by individual 'stars.' " Then, appealing to the "bottom line" of many corporate executives reading the *Journal,* he concluded: "The studies may offer lessons for executives on boosting productivity and innovation."[9]

Collaboration or working together demands "power sharing." Its goal is to create a kind of energy that gets exercised in ways that make the resulting energy bigger than the sum of its parts. This is another word for "synergy." Persons called husbands and wives learn this in what we call "marriage." It involves equality and equal power sharing. When this takes place, parents collaborate in bringing about a bigger reality than themselves: they birth another human into the world and go beyond their own interests by nurturing that child in ways of care. Indeed, power, must be shared equally if the marriage will work; thus the word "co-labor-ation." Persons called partners learn this in what we call a "small business." When one tries to co-opt the other's role in the relationship, conflict arises and the business will easily fail. Synergy demands a working together beyond competitive styles in order to pull off the greater good. People constituting nations learn this when they create forms of globalization that benefit as many as possible instead of the few. Collaboration is the stuff of healthy relationships at all levels of life. Synergy is the force behind as well as the consequence of collaboration.

Sofield and Juliano have learned from experience working with groups and those that may even call themselves "teams" that collaboration is a process that passes through four stages moving to full participative collaboration: (1) No collaboration: it is not a value because of existing dominating and controlling hierarchical models; (2) Obsession: we talk about it a lot but it remains at the level of rhetoric; (3) Ambivalence: we believe in it as a value but our fears override our efforts and we give in too easily when faced with difficulties; (4) Action: we commit ourselves to collaborate "as an operational norm" and agree "to continue even when it is difficult."[10]

Once a group is committed to the action step to make collaboration something more than talk, the members must develop relationships that will find them working together for some common good. Following our Power Chart and building on dynamics of affirmation from which challenge and even confrontation can flow without people "getting their back up," these relationships must work to ensure the two main characteristics of a community of care: the participants must feel they are free to share what they think will be for the common good and they must nurture their commitment to mutual affirmation and correction in ways that will engender trust. As we discovered in my own group as we discussed what would be demanded of us if we moved to a more collaborative model with those who were not direct members of the group, "the entire effort needed to be girded in an active effort on the part of all parties to develop an enduring ethos of trust, positive regard and respect."[11]

This kind of "ethos of trust" demands that all who are part of the effort must feel safe enough to share what they believe to be the best for the group project. In this sense, their freedom flows from their trust that they can use their talents in ways that honor their own gifts and support the common effort. "Collaboration is based on the ability to relate to others," Schofield and Juliano note, but then add: "and all relationships presuppose the capacity to trust. Trust requires an underlying belief that the other person is basically 'for' you and does not intend harm."[12] In other words, all persons in the relationship so function that they operate in non-competitive ways, which build the trust and contribute to the common project. When this trust is established and ensured through an understanding or some kind of agreement on a "ground rule" of mutual affirmation and confirmation of each other, combined with an agreed-upon way of addressing differences in the group through constructive confrontation and challenge, the members will have found a nonviolent way to bring about the change or results they desire. The process can be charted as follows:

communication ➔ common goals ➔ AGREEMENTS ➔
UNDERSTANDING ➔ COLLABORATION

Collaboration between Parents and Children and Other Traditionally Unequal Power Groups

When I give workshops on the Power Chart, invariably I will be challenged about my identification of "control" with negativity in our relationships by parents who feel that control is the only positive way they can discipline their children. "If we don't control them," is the sense, "they'll be out of control." Indeed the notion of control, in such a statement, is a two-edged sword. On the one hand it is simply a word that refers to a correct way of disciplining. In that sense "control" is a healthy way of relating. On the other hand, however, when "control" means that parents overpower their children via manipulation or domination, threats and coercion, it will not be healthy.

In my mind, constructive, healthy "control" means creating a "holding environment" of unconditional care that is expressed in ongoing affirmation and, from this, any kind of correction. When this is structured into family dynamics, freedom and trust will characterize the relationship between parents and children. This can occur with parents and children regarding concerns beyond the family as well as within the family itself. Nel Noddings gives a good example of how the model works in situations beyond the family itself in an incident of a child feeling aggrieved at school and a mother working to resolve the conflict. The pattern involves what she calls "receptivity":

> Suppose that a child of, say, eight years comes home from school angry. He storms into the kitchen and throws his books on the floor. His mother, startled, says, "What happened, honey?" (She resists the temptation to say something to the effect that "in this house we do not throw things.") The child says that his teacher is "impossible," "completely unfair," "mean," "stupid," and so on. His mother sympathizes and probes gently for what happened. Gradually, under the quiet influence of a receptive listener, the child calms down. As his mother sympathizes, he may even relax enough to say, "Well, it wasn't that bad," in answer to his mother's sympathetic outrage. Then the two may smile at each other and explore rational

solutions; they can speculate about faults, mistakes, and intentions. They can plot a course of action for the future. The child, accepted and supported, can begin to examine his own role in the incident and, perhaps, even suggest how he might have behaved differently.

The receptivity of the one-caring need not lead to permissiveness nor an abdication of responsibility for conduct and achievement. Rather, it maintains and enhances the relatedness that is fundamental to human reality.[13]

When it comes to creating a model of mutuality within families, when there is a sense of safety and security, all members of the family can create "ground rules" or agreements on basic disciplines to be followed, including rewards for adherence to these agreements and sanctions for violations. The agreements must be communicated in such a way that all will feel they have had their say in their creation. These agreements will outline basic assumptions and expectations flowing from the assumptions. These will get expressed in the "shoulds" and "should nots" for parents and children. Agreed-upon rewards/sanctions will be noted too.

When parents resist because of ongoing tensions in the family system, I suggest that they wait, making a kind of quiet or "truce" period. Then they invite all members to an away-from-home place, such as a restaurant where voices cannot be raised (like might happen around the kitchen table!). There the designated leader will quietly outline the destructive dynamics that are taking place in ways that benefit nobody. The leader will then suggest that there is another way that can be a "win/win" approach: an agreement to mutually affirm and correct as well as a kind of formalized contract among the members that will state assumptions and expectations with regard to key behaviors.

If parents say that such an approach is "impossible," I point to the increasing way other parental figures, e.g., teachers, are able to create a similar environment of collaboration with their students by "contractual learning." Interestingly, the approach is increasingly being used in businesses as well. The result is collaboration on the part of all.

Contractual learning as well as collaborative family discipline operates on the assumption that all parties are, by their identity as persons, empowered to influence each other; therefore all must be involved in agreeing to the processes that will take place. Because all will impact and be impacted by the others, the goal of such agreements between the parties is to move from the possibility of negative power relationships defining any of the "I ams" in the group and to create a positive environment of mutual respect and listening. Such a dialogue is the heart of what has traditionally been called "obedience." When obedience is shared listening and learning, it lays the groundwork for non-controlling and non-violent dynamics to define the discipline that takes place.

Collaboration:
The Empowering Care of a Successful Leader

Increasingly writers addressing the dynamics of successful leaders find a key component in the way they give up any need to control and find ways to empower others. In fact, a whole new form of leadership has evolved under the term "customer relationship management" (CRM). According to the website devoted to this form of organization, CRM "is a business strategy to select and manage customer relationships to optimize long-term value to an enterprise. CRM requires a customer-centric business philosophy and culture to support effective marketing, sales and service processes across all direct and indirect customer interaction channels."[14]

True leaders view themselves as servants or "midwives" of a birthing process: the realization of a common goal by all involved in the effort. One who has studied this style of effective leadership is Joe B. Tye, often called "America's Values Leader." In writing on "the paradox of servant leadership," he declares without reservation: "I've read hundreds of books and articles about leadership over the past several years (and written a few myself), and come away with this conclusion: the most effective leaders have great humility and truly do see themselves as servants rather than leaders. That is what makes them great leaders."[15]

Jesus showed clearly that the leadership of his followers had to differ from "the world's ways." He recalled how "they knew" how the "rulers of the Gentiles" operated in overpowering ways rather than empowering ones. Their "great ones" made their authority felt. So if their leadership would be modeled on his, they had to use power differently: "Whoever wishes to be great among you must be your servant, and whoever wishes to be first among you must be your slave" (Matt. 20:26–27).

Chapter Fourteen

The Power of Nonviolence

The Bad Rap about Nonviolence

In some groups, especially those trying to bring about social change, a temptation exists to work at institutional transformation in ways that often create more negativity on the part of others than healthy change. As we have defined it, violence is "any (un)intentional force that inflicts injury." If this be so, nonviolence will be "any (un)intentional force that creates healing." The energy within us powers all forms of violence as well as nonviolence; it's how we direct that force that makes all the difference. Nonviolence is strategic power exercised in ways that do not inflict pain.

A key obstacle to the practice of nonviolence is that it often is equated with a kind of passivity that seems able to be manipulated and exploited, dominated and controlled by others. Many of us have learned or have come to believe that the only way we can back up our bark is with a bite. In this sense I agree with Mary Lou Kownacki's conclusion that nonviolence "has a bad reputation." She goes on to equate the way many perceive it with the perception of a snake in the following story:

> t seems that in a certain village a snake had bitten so many people that few dared to go into the fields. Finally it was taken to a wise person who tamed the snake and persuaded it to practice the discipline of nonviolence.
>
> When the villagers discovered that the snake was harmless, they took to hurling stones at it and dragging it by its tail. Finally the badly battered and disillusioned snake crawled to the wise one and complained bitterly.
>
> "You've stopped frightening people," the wise one said, "and that's bad."
>
> The snake was incredulous. "But it was you who taught me to practice the discipline of nonviolence," the snake replied. "Oh," said the wise one, "I told you to stop hurting people, not to stop hissing."

Kownacki goes on to conclude: authentic nonviolence does not harm, but it does know when to hiss. It hisses loud and long at every system and structure that trods the weak and powerless underfoot. It hisses so strongly and with such persistence that governments topple and dictatorships dissolve.[1]

Practitioners of nonviolence impacted my formative years in dramatic, tragic events. I remember where I was when the news came that Mahatma Gandhi had been assassinated. I read it in the Fond du Lac, Wisconsin, paper as I got ready for my paper route. Some years later, I remember walking across Fourth Street in Milwaukee, in the heart of the African American community, when I heard that Dr. Martin Luther King Jr. had been assassinated. I remember, too, being in Washington, D.C., listening to the radio describing the troops of Ferdinand Marcos joining the thousands of their fellow citizens challenging his despotic rule. I also recall the joy I had watching the people pour over the Berlin Wall into the West after the collapse of the Soviet Union.

Building on what we have developed on our Power Chart thus far, I see *nonviolence* as a strategic, constructive force whose goal is the redressing of the abuse of power, the conflicts, the violence, and wars in and among us in ways that bring about greater care and love in our world. It involves a conscious choice to redirect power in our lives from whatever in, among, and around us may be violent toward a positive way of relating. It assumes, the Greeks would instruct us, that it involves an alternative use of power — from being a negative force in our relationships to a positive force.

Becoming Convinced That Nonviolence Is a More Effective Way of Using Power

While I might have been intellectually convinced about the power of nonviolence and its effectiveness in influencing others in their effort to change structures and unjust social arrangements, one of the most difficult, if not the most difficult, problems facing me when I tried to practice nonviolence involved my tendency to be violent in my methods. As I indicated in an earlier discussion, in working to bring about change, I was my own worst enemy. In this I was like the person Gandhi described about himself. He once said: "I have only three enemies. My favorite enemy, the one most easily influenced for the better, is the British nation. My second enemy, the Indian people, is far more difficult. But my most formidable opponent is a man named Mohandas K. Gandhi. With him, I seem to have very little influence."[2]

The *way* I used my own influence in the effort I sought to bring about social change was undermined by the means by which I did it. I dreamed of bringing about a world of nonviolence, peace, love, and compassion. Yet the way I was using my power, i.e., my "ability to influence," worked against that very goal. In my effort to bring about nonviolence, I was being violent. As I tried to bring about peace, I was anything but peace-filled, and as I envisioned a world defined by universal compassion, I was insensitive to the very ones I hoped could help bring it about.

Before I acknowledged "the exact nature of my wrongs," I feared if I changed from my more destructive and violent ways, I would be ineffective in bringing about the good I envisioned. In other words, I don't think I truly believed that a nonviolent approach to the elements described on the top level of our Power Chart could be possible. In the face of violence, I wondered, could another way bring about the change I so desired? It was only when I realized a nonviolent approach should be seen as a conscious strategy did I also realize that I would be able to be more effective in the way I exercised my power, my ability to influence, if I grounded myself in this strategy.

My realization that nonviolence is a strategy brought me to the work of Gene Sharp, once dubbed the "Clausewitz of nonviolent warfare." Sharp's strategic nonviolence is derived from a deep understanding of political power and its abuse by governments. Aware that they can keep their control to the degree they can impose obedience on their subjects, he saw that when citizens choose to withhold their cooperation with that control, governments lose not only their support but their legitimation. His strategies, related to "civilian-based defense" — organized nonviolent non-cooperation and defiance — were adopted as government policy by the Baltic States (Lithuania, Latvia, and Estonia) in their successful secession from the Soviet Union.[3]

Nonviolence and the Power of Gentleness

James Forest has pointed out a fascinating derivation of the word "nonviolence": "The Greek word [for nonviolence]...*praüs,* was used to describe a wild animal who had been tamed and made gentle; a horse that would accept a rider, a dog that would tend sheep. In the human sphere it refers to a person who disciplines himself to be gentle rather than severe, nonviolent rather than violent."[4]

Unfortunately, staying with the Greek *praüs,* the word has often been translated as "meek" with the result that people think they will be door-mats, wimps, and pushovers if they embrace such meekness. Therefore, it seems best to avoid the word "meek" and use words for *praüs* that speak more realistically to the way the word can be translated in our lives and behavior: non-controlling, non-abusive, and non-violent. Rather than being a power that overpowers those with whom we may differ in ways that make winners and losers, nonviolence becomes a power that seeks a win/win approach, empowering all toward a resolution of conflicts and discovery of collaborative efforts to bring about a greater good.

In other words, as John Henry Newman said, we become the gentle person. As such, by his definition, the gentleman or gentlewoman is "the one who does not inflict pain."

The nonviolent person uses power in a principled, disciplined way that does not overpower those with whom he or she disagrees but energizes them to think, feel, and act differently. Building on our Power Chart, we can agree with Blaine Lee in his book *The Power Principle:*

> Principle-centered power is the type of power possessed by Ma-hatma Gandhi and Nelson Mandela; power that inspires loyalty and devotion and that transcends time and place. It is based on trust and respect and survives long after the death of the one pos-sessing it. It uplifts and motivates those affected by it. It is a higher form of power — a better way.[5]

Nonviolence, such as that practiced by people like Gandhi in India, Mandela in South Africa, Martin Luther King Jr. in our country, and Daniel Dolci in Italy, begins in our "I am." It changes our hearts in the way we think, the way we emote, and the way we act. It demands an entirely new way of grounding ourselves and imaging others, feelings about conflict and ways to overcome the forces of control and violence in, among, and around us.

Nonviolence is a way of ordering our lives so that everyone will be empowered; it refers to people who discipline themselves to be gentle rather than severe. When this happens, gentleness becomes the positive face of nonviolence. On the one hand it does not control or create pain; on the other it shows care in a way that is grounded in deep respect and receptivity toward the other. In many ways gentleness is the way we fulfill the golden rule to deal with others as we would want them to deal with us. "We usually don't think of gentleness as a source of power," Blaine Lee notes. "Yet there's nothing as powerful as true gentleness. Such sensitivity requires that we really tune in to others."[6]

When I first found myself coming to the realization that I had to live from another way of using power (and in a nonviolent way) in order to be truly effective, I was driving to a town about seventy-five miles from Milwaukee with a coworker who had known me for years. He was very aware of my "MO," my manner of operating. My friend is quite cautious and reflective in his comments. He also had been studying and practicing nonviolence for years. At that time he was taking a course on nonviolence at Marquette University.

I was driving him to the town on a highway where the speed limit was 55 miles an hour and apparently I was not particularly attending to that. As we got rolling I said to him: "Art, I'm beginning to be fascinated by the theory and practice of nonviolence. So rather than using the hour it will take to arrive at our destination to just gossip about the community, why don't you tell me what you are learning."

He spent most of the next hour sharing with me the core theory of nonviolence. He noted how it was a form of directed power ordered to good for all who are conflicted or combatants. He clearly detailed how, as such, nonviolence is a force for good rather than harm. He showed how it heals broken relationships, restores trust, and builds up all those who may be on its practicing or receiving ends.

When it was almost an hour since we had begun our trip and turned onto the county highway from the state highway to take us to our destination, I said: "Art, you have known me for quite a few years. You have seen me function, and you have heard from others in the community how I operate. Now that you have given me so much of the theory related to nonviolence, how do you think I could become a practitioner of it?"

"Well, Mike," Art responded measuredly, "you might begin with your driving!"

We all have to begin somewhere. But any beginning involves an end of former ways and taking steps in another direction.

Almost twenty years ago I committed myself to begin a journey on the path of nonviolence. I find it has become a trip that will never end. I also find it to be one of the most challenging promises I have ever made. To continually work to be free of the violence in, among, and surrounding us in our culture and even our religions is one thing. But to work actively to change these in nonviolent ways is an even greater challenge. As I work on changing my own way of relating and becoming a nonviolent force for change, I find that this involves various dimensions of the way I interact with my immediate family and coworkers, the members of my mainly white, male, heterosexual, North American, clerical group, whose exercise of power has sometimes done violence to others, and the way I walk on the earth itself. Consequently, I must continually ask myself how I am living up to my commitment to give up my need to control others, to find ways of acting as a kind of filter that may cleanse the negative forms of power on the top part of the Power Chart without extending them beyond myself. I can do this by trying not to retaliate in the face of such provocations, by working to be nonviolent in the way I speak and think, and by living conscientiously and simply so that I do not deprive others of their right to live and exist, interrelatedly, on this planet.[7]

Nonviolent Truth-Telling

All civilized societies are based on the assumption that our relationships are grounded in truth-telling. However, when we have different values and outlooks regarding relationships at any level of the world, we will have different "truths." Oftentimes our convictions about our particular personal or group "truths" can result in quite violent ways of communicating them and thinking about others who disagree with them.

We need to tell our truth in the way outlined by the Letter to the Ephesians: (1) practice the truth (2) in care (3) in order to build up the body (Eph. 4:15). In a nation divided into combatants in a "culture war" on the "left" and "right" politically, economically, and religiously, I found a column by Rev. Richard John Neuhaus, a neoconservative quite hopeful that something might be different once we become aware of how deeply destructive our differing ideologies can be when we define them in terms of "the truth." Commenting on the findings of Edward Shils, which showed similarities in beliefs and attitudes between the radical ideological right and the extreme ideological left, Neuhaus opined that, while Shils drew his examples from Nazism and Communism, "the analysis applies to situations of ideological and political polarization more generally." He outlined eight characteristics describing how this polarization leads to incivility and uncharitableness among us:

1. Extreme hostility to "outgroups." You are either for us or against us. Dialogue or civil conversation with the "enemy" is betrayal.

2. Complete submissiveness to "ingroups." Our party and its leaders are to be supported without question. Criticism of our side is breaking ranks, and breaking ranks is treason.

3. All relationships are subordinated to the criterion of what will advance the "cause."

4. The most important thing to know about the world is that it is divided by the conflict between them and us.

5. Purely theoretical ideas that do not clearly serve the cause are to be repressed.

6. The expression of sentiment is a sign of weakness.

7. We and our group can survive only by the manipulation of others, who are there to be manipulated.

8. The triumph of the cause will result in a harmonious world without conflict.

Upon noting these points, Neuhaus concludes: "There is a seductive pleasure in hating, and hating absolutely. To judge by some of the vicious messages received in this office — and, I am sure, received also by those on the other side of controverted issues — more people than we would like to think are susceptible to that seduction. Securing the bonds of civility within which we engage our differences is a never-ending task."[8] To this I can only say "Amen."

The third part of our triad of "practicing the truth in care in order to build up the body" invites us to ask: Why am I practicing the truth in this way? Am I talking like this in order to help bring about a real difference in the person or the situation? Is it geared to change the dynamics of the relationship in a way that will bring about the common good? For instance, when I gossip about the failings of another I may be telling the truth; but if my communicating in this way is not grounded in care or affirmation, it's not likely that anyone or anything will change.

I used to say many things about dynamics in the institutional church and its leaders that were negative. However, seldom if ever did I speak from a loving heart. Neither did I show care toward them in the way Jesus said we were to love our "enemy" or the one with whom we were at odds. Even less did I do this *in order* to build up the body. Indeed, I often did it to "build up" Michael Crosby and, in so doing, become confirmed in my own righteousness. Nothing changed.

Then I began to ask myself: What good happens when you do it this way? How can they possibly change when you never address them directly? This led me to begin writing letters to my economic and political leaders as well as to those Vatican officials whose way of discipline and governance I felt the need to challenge. In the process of "practicing the truth in care" in the way I would write my letters to them, disagreeing with this or that stance, I found myself changing my way of thinking and feeling about them. It even led to a response once in a while, indicating they had heard my concerns and would pray for me.

Other Ways of Nonviolence

A key strategy of those who have practiced nonviolence over the years — all the way from Jesus to Gandhi to Dr. Martin Luther King Jr. — has been the attempt to disarm one's opponents through the tactic of shame. Jesus invited his followers to go the "extra mile" and to "give one's cloak" i.e., go naked in a society where nakedness was the shame of the beholder, Gandhi resisted the control of a nation composed of citizens who were fastidious and civilized and thus lost their desire for the domination of another people, while King kept to the higher moral ground in his dealings with his opponents, thus delegitimizing their justification for the laws that, until that time, had sustained the violence perpetrated on non-whites in the United States.

In honor/shame cultures, challenge and riposte define all relationships and, therefore, the exercise of power within them. Especially when someone "attacks" in this way, the person is not so doing seeking an explanation for another's behavior. Rather this involves a challenge to one's core identity and identifiers in some way. In some cultures a riposte is the only honorable way one is expected to respond to such challenges. However, the challenge/riposte only escalates as the way to avoid shame and promote the honor of one's self or one's group.

I have found that to avoid escalating conflict is to disarm the one who is angrily challenging or "attacking" me for something I have said or done. And a very effective way to disarm him or her is simply to apologize.

Because we have become accustomed to "apologies that are not apologies," we must be very honest in our apology if it is to be truly disarming. It isn't good enough to say: "I'm sorry if I offended you." "I'm sorry if you misunderstood what I was trying to say." "I'm sorry that you are upset." Instead we should be able, at this point, to simply say "I'm sorry" and mean it. I now can truly say "I'm sorry" and mean it insofar as I am sorry that whatever I did brought about negativity in the relationship.

Another way many thousands of people in the Roman Catholic tradition have found to help them on the path of nonviolence is to become committed to implement six practices outlined by Pax Christi in its "Vow of Nonviolence." At every workshop I give, I make it a point to invite the participants to consider making this pledge. However, after clarifying the fact that the "Vow of Nonviolence" is not a vow in the canonical

sense but that it is something that should be seriously made, I also cau-
tion them not to be too quick in making such a commitment but to do
so gradually since there are many steps that must be redirected that keep
us on the top part of the Power Chart before we commit ourselves to
take the steps on the bottom part. The vow reads:

> Recognizing the violence in my own heart, yet trusting in the
> goodness and mercy of God, I vow for one year to practice the
> nonviolence of Jesus, who taught us in the Sermon on the Mount:
> "Blessed are the peacemakers, for they shall be called the sons and
> daughters of God. . . . You have learned how it was said, 'You must
> love your neighbor and hate your enemies,' but I say to you, 'Love
> your enemies, and pray for those who persecute you.' In this way,
> you will be daughters and sons of your Creator in heaven."
>
> Before God the Creator and the Sanctifying Spirit, I vow to carry
> out in my life the love and example of Jesus
>
> - by striving for peace within myself and seeking to be a peace-
>   maker in my daily life;
> - by accepting suffering rather than inflicting it;
> - by refusing to retaliate in the face of provocation and violence;
> - by persevering in nonviolence of tongue and heart;
> - by living conscientiously and simply so that I do not deprive
>   others of the means to live;
> - by actively resisting evil and working nonviolently to abolish
>   war and the causes of war from my own heart and from the face
>   of the earth.
>
> God, I trust in Your sustaining love and believe that just as You
> gave me the grace and desire to offer this, so You will also bestow
> abundant grace to fulfill it.[9]

Finally, our individual efforts at nonviolence will be immeasurably
strengthened when we join synergistically with others toward living nonviolently. This demands that we find a support system to affirm and
challenge us in our efforts when we are succeeding as well as when we
may be failing to be effective practitioners of nonviolence. A friend and
co-worker of mine who is dedicated to nonviolence, Dominican Kathy
Long, insists that in our practice of nonviolence "community is essential; it sustains, encourages and nourishes. Each individual makes choices

within the context of a community of resistance to pursue truth and justice." In the context of community, she insists that "nonviolent wisdom" will flow

> ...from the collective experience of trusting and sharing in the effort to counter violence. This weaving of relationships in nonviolent dissent nurtures the seeds of compassion, engaging persons in understanding, forgiveness and mindfulness. A well-formed community finds its strength in one another as the struggle intensifies. Good skills will foster the building of community and empower all in nonviolent dissent.[10]

When a community of nonviolence is characterized by such internal forms of affirmation and correction, it can become an even more effective instrument for the effectuation of peace.

Chapter Fifteen

The Recipe for Making Peace

On December 1, 2000, a full-page advertisement in *USA Today* announced: "You can buy Happiness, Love, Health, Prosperity, and Peace. But only until December 31st." It was an ad for differently etched Waterford "millennium toasting flutes"; the names were secondary. Later, on September 23, 2001, a full-page of the *New York Times* ran nothing below the masthead on page A16 but one sentence in the middle of it: "Imagine all the people living life in peace." I kept looking on the previous page and the following one for its sponsor. It remained anonymous.

Given that we have already reflected on dynamics among us that indicate we are a nation addicted to violence (Bob Herbert) and that we just don't care (Peggy Noonan) and that we are indifferent to what other people think of us regarding our violence and carelessness, it's a little hard to "imagine all the people living life in peace." While we would like to think of ourselves as a peace-able people, to have us be characterized as peacemakers by others, especially as a nation, is almost unimaginable. Indeed, too often the complaint of Jeremiah the Prophet seems more apropos of our situation: "We have heard a cry of panic, of terror, and no peace" (Jer. 30:5) or, in the more familiar grief-stricken passage about the hardness of our hearts:

> From the least to the greatest of them,
> everyone is greedy for unjust gain;
> and from prophet to priest,
> everyone deals falsely.
> They have treated the wound of my people carelessly,
> saying, "Peace, peace," when there is no peace.
> (Jer. 6:13–14)

Improbable as it might be, it does seem quite unimaginable, but not yet impossible, to wonder how we might become people of peace: peacemakers in our individual, communal, and collective lives. If the ultimate challenge for us is to become peacemakers in a way that finds us united

148

under God as God's sons and daughters and, therefore, as brothers and sisters, this challenge invites us to probe how this peace might be *made*. In writing my book on the Beatitudes of Jesus in Matthew's Gospel, it became clear to me that the seventh beatitude — "Blessed are the peacemakers, they will be called children of God" (Matt. 5:9) — like all the other beatitudes, involves dynamics that must be rejected (called "stumbling blocks") and dynamics that must be developed if we are to receive the blessing described by the particular beatitude.

From this perspective it becomes clear that "blessed are the peacemakers" involves a recipe for *making peace*. As such, the making of peace, like all recipes that are made, must follow certain prescriptions: there are ingredients that must never be part of the process and others that are essential.

When I give workshops on ways we can move from controlling dynamics in our lives and relationships to those grounded in care, I begin by sharing a recipe that is easy to make. It's called "Catalina Chicken." It takes four ingredients: a jar of fat-free Catalina salad dressing, a jar of low-sugar apricot preserves, a bag of onion soup mix, and some chicken breasts. You create a marinade, soak the chicken breasts, and then bake at 350 degrees for 30–35 minutes. From this I explain that "making peace" in ourselves, our communities, and our world involves a recipe: there are ingredients you must never add to the mix and ingredients that are essential. Given our Power Chart, I think we can find some key ingredients that should be put into the mix that would *make peace* and some significant elements that should be avoided like the plague at all levels of life, starting with ourselves.

Making Peace with Ourselves

In "Everything Depends on Your Peace," the Buddhist monk Thich Nhat Hanh writes:

> We need to find an inner peace which makes it possible for us to become one with those who suffer, and to do something to help our brothers and sisters, which is to say, ourselves. I know many young people who are aware of the real situation of the world and who are filled with compassion. They refuse to hide themselves in artificial peace, and they engage in the world in order to change the society. They know what they want, yet after a period of involvement they become discouraged. Why? It is because they lack deep, inner peace, the kind of peace they can take with them into their life of action.

Our strength is not in weapons, money, or power. Our strength is in our peace, the peace within us. This peace makes us indestructible. We must have peace while taking care of those we love and those we want to protect.

I have recognized this peace in many, many people. Most of their time and effort is spent protecting the weak, watering the trees of love and understanding everywhere. They belong to various religious and cultural backgrounds. I do not know how each of them came to their inner peace, but I have seen it in them.[1]

I am not one to second-guess someone like Thich Nhat Hanh. Although he writes, "I do not know how each of them came to their inner peace," I believe that I have discovered the key aspects necessary for any recipe that will make peace in our lives.

After I give my recipe for Catalina Chicken, I ask the participants to think about someone they know — in their family of origin, among their coworkers or professional colleagues, or members of some association — who they would say has discovered the "recipe for peace." How did they "make peace" in their hearts and with others? I then ask them to reflect quietly on what they think these persons had to do (and not do) to make peace in their individual lives.

After a few minutes I ask them to write down two or three "ingredients" that have enabled them to come to this point in their lives. What might they have avoided doing in order to "make peace" with themselves and others? What did they make sure they did in order to be called a peace-able person?

When they have noted these I ask them to share their "recipe" with their tablemates. Then I ask: "Are you finding any common ingredients?" "Are there any things that should never be put into the mix?" Then I ask them to write these down. When all the groups have finished, they summarize their small group's recipe for making peace in our individual lives.

In the twenty plus years that I have been doing this the recipe has always remained the same. Two ingredients always stand apart from other options. One might be considered the wrong ingredient that spoils the recipe; the other is the only positive ingredient that it takes to make peace with one's self. The obstacle or stumbling block that must always be removed and never be part of a recipe of "peace" is "the need to control." The other ingredient, the one that is essential for peace in every heart, is simple enough in itself but one that often takes a lifetime to achieve: "accepting one's self for who one is." In other words, personally speaking:

"I accept myself for who I am and give up the need to control others." Conversely this involves accepting others for who they are and nonviolently keeping them from trying control our "I am." Free of the need to control and accepting ourselves for who we are, we have discovered the recipe for making peace with ourselves. At the same time, we share this recipe with others in the way we refuse to try to control them and accept them for who they are. But more on this below.

When we commit ourselves to the effort of not trying to control others, we are well on the path of deep spirituality. Why? Because at the heart of every spirituality we find the kenotic or self-emptying dimension. It may receive different names, such as humility, detachment, renunciation, relinquishing, or "letting go"; however, when we truly give up our tendency to control and commit ourselves to the process of allowing others to be free of this need in each of us, we will be ready to move more rapidly on the spiritual journey.

St. Francis of Assisi grasped the heart of this insight when he spoke against himself and his followers seeking or acquiring wealth in any form (power, property, or titles): "if we had possessions, we would need arms for our protection. For disputes and lawsuits usually arise out of them, and, because of this, love of God and neighbor are greatly impeded. Therefore, we do not want to possess anything in this world."[2] Having leads to claiming; conflicts over claims leads to control and violence. Francis sought to give up whatever might disturb his peace, including his inheritance itself. When the *Wall Street Journal* features articles on "Making Peace over Money" to address "Family Battles over Wealth,"[3] and "How to Keep Peace among Heirs,"[4] dealing with issues of inheritance, it's too bad that Francis's wisdom has not yet captured people's imaginations.

Secondly, besides giving up our need or desire to control others and events, when we find ourselves being free of others' need to control us and accept ourselves, as the beloved "I am" that is very good, we no longer give power to those others to control us, be it in our thoughts, emotions, or behavior. Even if this takes entering into therapy or residential treatment, when we can simply say, in the midst of all the forces trying to control our thinking and actions, "I am who I am," we become truly free. We find ourselves embracing the divine image within us. This brings us to peace; the recipe has been a success.

This, I would tell Thich Nhat Hanh, seems to be the inner recipe we all learn in different versions of how all people can come "to their inner peace."

Making Peace in Our Groups and Families

I was struck by an incident that occurred during the Second Iraqi War, in November 2006. Seemingly in the Christmas mood, a couple in Pagosa Springs, a small town two hundred miles southwest of Denver, placed a four-foot wreath shaped like a peace symbol in front of their house. In response to concerns from their neighbors, who found the peace symbol politically "divisive," they were threatened with fines of $25 a day unless they removed the wreath. They refused. When the issue became national news because other townspeople began putting up their own wreaths in the section of town where the original wreath appeared, the issue was quietly tabled.[5] When I read about the situation as it developed and, especially, how nonviolently it ended when more neighbors erected their own wreaths, it was a mini-repetition of the way the Danes decided to wear yellow arm bands proclaiming that they too were Jews, to save the real Jews from deportation during World War II.

In my own life I have discovered — the hard way, unfortunately — that the "recipe for peace" in our relationships with each other must always preclude any dynamics that would bring about a break in peace. I have also learned — the hard way — that, unless we "cut out" the kind of thinking about our partners, spouses, and close relationships that put nations on a "war footing," we will easily find ourselves on the path to war rather than the way to peace.

Any marriage counselor or conflict resolutions specialist will tell us that all breaks in such relationships are accompanied by certain attitudes the "warring parties" develop. Both sides see (1) the other(s) in the conflict as diabolical or evil, (2) themselves as having the resources to "win," as well as (3) morally right[eous]. However, (4) they consider only the negatives about their opponents and (5) show little or no care or empathy for what they think, feel, or desire. Overall, a disinterested observer would say that (6) the whole situation is quite irrational.[6]

Nevertheless, if such attitudes are not checked at the door, the marriage or relationship involved will lead to war and further from peace.

When the parties involved become aware of such dynamics or realize their relationship is being destroyed, they can do one of two things: descend further into the conflicted state in ways that will result in a break, possible hate, and ultimately indifference, or they can commit themselves to resolve their conflicts and make a renewed agreement to create the grounds for peace rather than "irreconcilable differences."

I have found that, just as individual peace has two ingredients as do wars among peoples (immediate cause and underlying causes), so, making peace in our marriages demands the creation of the covenant of care that I discussed earlier. While it may take various forms, it always revolves around the main components that constitute a community of care: the parties must agree to mutually affirm each other and be affirmed by each other as well as agree, building on the affirmation, to mutually challenge each other and be open to be challenged by each other.

Grounded in this kind of care the dynamics for "making peace" can overpower any of the stumbling blocks that so often lead to wars among nations, divorce in marriages, and walk-outs in families.

Recipes for Peace amid Cultural Differences

Years ago a friend of mine was working at a school in Montana serving the people of the Cheyenne and Crow nations. He came upon two first-graders fighting with each other. He broke it up and then asked what had led to their battle. "She's my enemy," the one said. "Why," asked my friend Gary. "She's a Cheyenne," came the first girl's reply. "Well you're our enemy too," said the Cheyenne. "How can you say that to each other," Gary asked, "you're not fighting with me." "Why should we be fighting with you," asked one. "Well, I'm a white man," said Gary. "You are?" they asked incredulously. When he affirmed what he had said, they replied together: "Well, then, you'll get yours too!"

Children learn how to "go to war" based on underlying or ideological constructs combined with a precipitating cause. While such dynamics must be avoided if there will be peace among nations and any other parties that may be heading toward conflict, it's equally important that we discover the building blocks that will ensure peace within our borders and beyond them.

At the level of disparate groups, a critical way to bring otherwise potentially conflicted parties to greater harmony and peaceableness involves finding ways of bringing otherwise opposite groups together in common cause. As noted earlier, I discovered this when I found myself conflicted with Dale Olen. However, the principle is applicable globally, as when, after a 2005 earthquake in Pakistan and India, the two conflicted nations opened their borders to rush aid to the victims whose tragedy went beyond previous divisions between the nations involved. Sad to say, it also may be a reason why so many historically conflicted Islamic groups have found common cause in their resistance to what they perceive to be U.S. incursions in their way of life.

Shortly after 9/11/01, I read a wonderful op-ed piece from the *Los Angeles Times:* "Say 'Peace' to a Muslim and Mean It." It told the story of James Lee Walker, an Episcopal priest. Wanting to do something to bring about a lessening of tensions that arose from the terrorist attacks, he found himself turning into the driveway of an Islamic Center. There he met two men who told him the leaders of the Center were away. He asked them if they'd give him a tour of the mosque. When it was finished, one of the young men asked: "May I ask you a favor? Is it all right if we take a photo of you?"

"A photo?" he wondered. "Of me? Why?"

"Sure," he replied, "Where do you want me, up against this wall?"

"Actually, I have one more favor to ask. Would you mind if I stood in the photo with you.?"

The priest must have looked as confused as he felt, because the young man laughed as he explained: "Since Tuesday, my mother has been calling and calling, crying to me to come home. She tells me, 'Walk to Mexico if you have to, but get on a plane and come home to Morocco. Soon all the Christians in the Untied States will rise up and slay every Muslim they can find! I want you safe!' "

Father Walker shook his head in dismay and said, "That's not going to happen here."

"I know," the young man countered. "But when my mother sees me next to a priest, she will believe I'm safe."

So they stood together, arms around each other's shoulders, the young Moroccan who prays to Allah and the middle-aged priest who celebrates Christ's resurrection at Mass. They looked into the camera to allay the fears of a mother far away.

"Say peace," said the photographer, before he snapped the picture. They did. And they meant it.[7]

Another recipe for peace among diverse peoples can be found when they intermingle, when they get mixed up. Ashutosh Varshney, a political scientist at the University of Michigan, discovered that the reason why some cities in India were peaceful rather than torn apart by ethnic and religious violence could be traced to the way they had integrated themselves socially, politically, and economically. What he found was that ethnically integrated organizations — including business associations, trade unions, professional groups, political parties, sports clubs — are far less vulnerable to conflict.[8]

Still another way nations and other groups can make peace with others beyond themselves is based on developing characteristics already noted on the bottom of our Power Chart, especially by working together in international groups. Such collaboration is based on mutually agreed upon "covenants" aimed to ensure peace among their signators. Again, the assumption rests on people making such agreements from a collective agreement as to their binding effect.

Justice in Our Structures:
No Peace without Right Relations

The motto inscribed on the coat-of-arms of Pope Pius XII was "Peace Is the Work of Justice." Since justice is defined by right relationships among individuals, communities, and groups, there can be no peace within any of these if they are based on unequal power relationships. Something will be wrong and conflict will result.

The very day I was putting some finishing touches on this chapter on peace, the *New York Times* reported that one of Edward Hicks's *The Peaceable Kingdom* paintings was going to be auctioned at Sotheby's in early 2006.[9] The report made me realize that, while somebody might be ready to purchase this painting, all of us are challenged to invest in the vision it is meant to portray: somehow we are to find a way to live on this earth of animate and inanimate creation in a way that will find us not just free of war but productively working together. The *Peaceable Kingdom* will be one of reconciliation and right relationships between and among all.

In a previous section I talked about reconciliation demanding the interplay of repentance for wrongdoing and forgiveness for the wrong done. An assumption that grounds all efforts at reconciliation is that the wrong will be righted and that broken relationships will be restored via right relations. "Right relations" is another phrase connoting justice. Another phrase for justice connected to "right relations," is "equity (if not outright equality) in power-sharing."

From our chart, it should be clear that authentic reconciliation among conflicted parties involves some kind of equality in their sharing of power. Otherwise someone or some group vis-à-vis an alternate person or group will be overpowering in a way that disempowers the other. This demands reordered relationships moving toward equal power sharing.

Equality in power sharing is another word for justice. Until some basic equity in power is structured into our personal, communal, and collective relationships, there will be unfairness and injustice. Where unfairness and injustice reign or rule the power dynamic, peace will be impossible to achieve.

During the peak of South African apartheid, as groups called for reconciliation, it became clear to me and to others that there could be no reconciliation because of apartheid itself. By its very definition "apartheid" stood for unequal power relationships. Until this institutionalized abuse was reordered, there could be no justice and therefore no peace.

Today, as we find other forms of apartheid tearing apart efforts to bring about a "Peaceable Kingdom," we need to realize as well that there can be no peace without justice, no rest until structured wrongs are turned into right relationships. One of the greatest forms of apartheid in the United States and among the family of nations is revealed in the growing disparity between rich and poor. In 2005, major disseminators of information finally acknowledged the nation's increasing class divide in the print media. It began with a *Wall Street Journal* series on "Challenges to the American Dream." One of its features declared: "As Rich-Poor Gap Widens in the U.S. Class Mobility Stalls."[10] There followed a ten-part series called "Class Matters" in the *New York Times*. One of the pieces showed that, because of tax laws, the very richest were leaving even the rich behind, not so much at the expense of the poor, but those in the middle class. In the U.K. as well as the "developing world," we find similar inequality.[11] The *Economist* noted a 2007 report by the Asian Development Bank (ADB) showing that "income inequality has increased over the past decade or so in 15 of the 21 countries it has studied. It concluded "inequality in many Asian countries could now be nudging Latin American levels if measured on a comparable basis."[12]

Given such disparities at the macro-levels as well as micro-levels in our nation, why would there be no outrage? Why the indifference? If it would be a kind of cultural psychic numbing, as we discussed earlier, I think it would be understandable if still not acceptable. However, another piece of data shows a deeper, more culturally sanctioned violence that not only seems to tolerate this disparity but also unconsciously supports it.

Such lack of care may arise from the fact that a very large number of citizens of this country actually believe they now are the beneficiaries of the inequities in the system, or will be one day: 19 percent of Americans believe they have incomes within the top 1 percent while another 20 percent believe they will be within the top 1 percent some day.[13] Why challenge data that show that the 500 wealthiest men earn all together more than the 416 million poorest people in the world if you think that whatever enabled them to become so rich will someday happen to you? Returning to our Power Chart, it is not so much that people are indifferent to the plight of the victims of these arrangements; they just "don't care" as long as they think they might also become beneficiaries of these unjust structures. And if people would rise up to protest such inequity, they can be quickly suppressed; the military is on the side of those interests.

When Hurricane Katrina hit the southern states, any blinders were ripped off and any defenses justifying why things were not as bad as had been reported became clear in the pictures in the morning papers and the stark stories on the evening news. As an op-ed piece in *Business Week* stated:

> What the images Americans saw on the evening news revealed about who was dying, who was trapped, who was without food, who was drinking contaminated water — and, yes, who was looting — should give us all pause. Is this what the pioneers of the Civil Rights movement fought to achieve — a society in which black people were as trapped and isolated by their poverty as they were by segregation laws?

The author, Mark D. Naison, a professor at New York's Fordham University, concluded: "If September 11 showed the power of a nation united in response to a devastating attack, Hurricane Katrina exposed the fault lines of a region — and a nation — rent by profound social divisions. Fixing New Orleans' breached levees without repairing that greater divide will leave only half the job done." [14]

Before other nations would be able to stop their finger-pointing at the economically induced racial apartheid in our own nation, they had to face their own divides — especially France, when virtually every one of its major urban areas experienced uprisings of the Islamic minorities that have been kept isolated from the mainstream. [15] At the same time, the rich nations were unable to agree on basic Millennium Goals that would have begun to address the growing disparity between the rich and poor nations themselves. If, since 1990, more than 130 million people were able to emerge from extreme poverty, the fact remains that the situation has worsened in eighteen countries and 10 million children die annually from avoidable causes. [16]

If poverty is economic violence, peace will be impossible until greater justice among the divided groups takes place.

If poverty is non-participation in decision making, then peace will be equally impossible until greater justice among divided groups takes place in the institutional church as well. This was the thrust of my remarks some years ago when I called for a "Kairos Moment in the Catholic Church." I based my remarks on the "Kairos Document" of South African theologians during the country's political and economic apartheid. They stated there could be no reconciliation between blacks, coloreds, and whites until such groups had basic equality. Consequently, I stated, in the Roman Church, with its parallel ecclesiastical and clerical apartheid, there can be no reconciliation and, therefore, no peace until the church finds a way to balance the power of ordination with the power of baptism. I stated that "ecclesiastical apartheid"

> ...is represented in the gulf between clergy and laity, women and men, and gays and straights. In my theological reflection on the use of the word *kairos* (i.e., special opportunity) in Luke's Gospel, I will suggest that the abuse of authority and violence against lay people, specifically women and gays, by our highest clerical leaders is exactly what Jesus, the layman, said must be changed by accepting the Good News of God's reign, which he preached.[17]

Until this communion is achieved, the greeting of every bishop to the people at Mass will sound somewhat hollow: "Peace be with you."

Chapter Sixteen

Growing in Love

I began fulltime ministry in 1968, "the year that made us who we are," *Newsweek* declared on its November 19, 2007, cover. I know 1968 had a great influence on me. So I still like listening to Dionne Warwick reminding us that "what the world needs now is love, sweet love" and to recall the unity we felt when we came to the aid of people suffering from famine in parts of Africa — inspired by the song: "We Are the World."

In 1992 Andrew Lloyd Weber released a song that has become one of my favorites as well as one of the most popular songs of his career: "Love Changes Everything." As one listens to its lyrics, it becomes clear that, in the process of love changing *everything* it is because love *has first changed us.* As a result "nothing in the world will ever be the same."[1]

While we might "just love" to hear this song and become enraptured by its lyrics about the way love can change *everything,* I find that very few people honestly ground themselves in this conviction, even people of faith who believe that God is love and that, with God's love, everything can change, even our negative ways of relating.

One of the best examples of how people found this to be the case came in a story I read about three Protestant ministers, Gerrit Scott Dawson, Marcus Atha, and E. Cary Simonton. These men have been friends from their youth and have made it a point every year to spend extended periods with each other, apart from their wives. Deeply committed to the Lord and to justice, they have had many discussions and arguments in their effort to be faithful.

One time their sharing became deeply personal to the point that Gerrit said in so many words, "I guess there's no reason for me to be here." Broken, sick, and disgusted at the way things had developed, the three went home. Only then did each of them come to be challenged and convicted by the powerful and promising words found in Paul's Letter to the Romans: "I am convinced that neither death, nor life, nor angels, nor rulers, nor things present, nor things to come, nor powers, nor height, nor depth, nor anything else in all creation, will be able to separate us from the love of God in Christ Jesus our Lord" (Rom. 8:38). They discovered that they had allowed themselves to be separated around theological and personal differences but that this very separation was keeping them from God's love. Nothing "in all creation" should have led to that point. However, it did. But then, because they believed in the power of this passage and the power of God's love in their relationship, the wounds were healed. As Cary Simonton noted: "That is the mark of Christian community. If that 'mark' were not present, then I'm not sure we would be either 'community' or 'Christian.'"

Cary admitted that it "took a few months for us to heal, to listen to one another, and to learn from one another again, but we did get there and we learned an important lesson."[2] They had allowed something other than God to separate them; now, in God and God's love, they could be reconciled and restored in their love for each other.

The Nature of Love

Some neuroscientists at the University College of London have begun researching the idea that there may be a "brain wave that's known as love."[3] For her part Rutgers anthropologist Helen Fisher believes that romantic love itself has three phases — lust, attraction, and attachment — and that each of these phases manifests a "distinct pattern of brain activity."[4] If it can be shown from science that, at least for humans, love is the ultimate energy in our world, as such it constitutes the core energy of our lives.

Besides being the core energy of human beings, love is also that power into which the other energies in the universe also ultimately merge. It brings us, as the priest and paleontologist Pierre Teilhard de Chardin wrote, to be part of "the most universal, the most tremendous and the most mysterious of the cosmic forces. . . . Love by definition is the word we use for attractions of a personal nature. It is love which forms and will increasingly form, in its pure state, the material of human energy."[5]

Besides being the ultimate energy encapsulating all core energies of our heart as well as that core energy that unites us with the power of the universe itself, it seems clear that love will be the standard by which we leave our heritage to those who will survive us. I discovered this fact by reading accounts of the victims of the various flights and those in the World Trade Center's Twin Towers, a few weeks after September 11, 2001. The messages, delivered by cell phone, e-mail, and even by voicemail, are indelible testimonies that, in the evening of our life, love will be all that matters and that, to those who matter in our lives, our only legacy to them will be our love itself. This will be the way we will continue to live in their hearts, their thoughts, their feelings, and their memories. One of these victims was Brian Sweeney, thirty-eight, of Barnstable, Massachusetts. He was a passenger on Flight no. 175. Shortly before it crashed into the World Trade Center's South Tower, he left a message for his wife, Julie, on their answering machine. He said: "Hey Jules, it's Brian. I'm on a plane and it's hijacked and it doesn't look good. I just wanted to let you know that I love you and I hope to see you again. If I don't please have fun in life and live your life the best you can. Know that I love you and no matter what, I'll see you again."[6]

Nurturing Self-Love

"Love your neighbor as yourself," found in the Jewish scriptures and used by Jesus in the Christian scriptures, has often been interpreted more from our need to love "our neighbor" rather than loving ourselves. However, if we are able to truly love ourselves in a dynamic of affirmation and acceptance of ourselves, from which flows any challenge to ourselves (rather than the other way around, which usually indicates some degree of self-hatred), we are well on our way to a healthy self-love.

As the bottom of our Power Chart shows, as we would apply it to loving ourselves, such love means we also trust ourselves and feel free to be our unique "I am." We have a healthy sense of self and exude a confidence that is grounded rather than a kind of false bravado. We are humble insofar as we accept the good and not-so-good of our past and present; we live in this truth. A healthy self-love is nurtured in caring relationships of affirmation and correction. It is energized when others trust us and allow us to be free. Self-love is another word for self-acceptance. As Dale Olen writes of our formation into self-love and self-acceptance:

> The more positive and unconditional the messages you received in childhood, the more you accept yourself. The key to positive self-esteem lies in being loved by parents without conditions. You are good just because you exist — and not because you got straight As, did the dishes without complaining, or won the student body elections. If you were loved without having to prove you were a worthwhile creature, then you have one leg up on the skill of self-acceptance.[7]

When I love myself I embrace the good and the not-so-good about my "I am." I make friends with my real self and my shadow self: who I really am as well as what I hide from the world's view. I also find ways to integrate my shadow self with my true self. The power to do this can come from no one or no force outside myself. While outside forces can influence the process in ways that make this task of self-love to be easier or harder, in the last analysis I must wake up one morning after many sleepless nights of self-paralysis to say: "I am good." When we find ourselves "good enough," we have accepted ourselves without comparing ourselves to anyone. We have enveloped ourselves in love. Realizing that love is an energy, we come to realize that this power is grounded in our very "I am." In this sense Olen writes:

> At your heart lie fundamentally good energies, created in you from the beginning. These are not powers that are earned. They come with your existence. They are built in. These energies or movements continually urge you toward freedom and love. They call you to live fully, to live in peace, contentment, and joy. These energies cannot be taken from you in any way. You are the energies of your heart. Since they are fundamentally good, so are you.[8]

Many of us spend years on this journey into self-love; for most of us we are especially challenged to address it in our midyears. It's during this time that I had to free myself from being controlled by others' thinking, feeling, and emotions about my "I am," to an embrace of myself as someone good. While the pain that was involved in this process was real, the result was worth the effort. Thus, to love myself is to allow the energy of my "I am" to believe in myself deeply and to nurture my "I am" in affirmation and correction when I turn away from loving myself rightly or others justly.

I once met someone who had been in recovery from alcoholism after her extended time in treatment. I asked: "What is the most powerful thing that happened to you in treatment?" Without blinking an eye she responded: "I am loved unconditionally. This has empowered me to love myself. Before, I had a 'hole in my heart.' Now that hole is filled with love for myself. It has empowered me to love others without conditions."

A few days after being told that the realization of being loved unconditionally had become the most important insight this woman gained from therapy, I was on a plane thinking about her words. I found myself asking: "What does it mean to love another unconditionally?" This led me to pull out a piece of paper. I wrote on it: "Unconditional Love." Under those words I wrote: "No conditions on the love." And under that, "No conditions on the relationship."

Then I wrote: "When there are conditions on the love and relationship they get expressed in various ways: 'I will love you, if you...'; 'I will love you because you...'; 'I will love you until you...'; 'I will love you when you....'" These also can get articulated as 'but if you,' 'only because you,' 'not until you,' or 'but when you' as qualifiers on the love. The more I wrote my thoughts down, the clearer it became: when we put conditions on our love, they act as obstacles to the possibility of unconditional love. Furthermore, each one of these conditions in our relationships represents subtle and not-too-subtle ways we try to control the other. Each one of these conditions also restricts a healthy love of our self. Relationships defined by conditions are also defined by control.

Some time after meeting the woman who gave me this insight, I received a call from a young man I have known since he was born. I had met his parents at a meeting when I was a young priest and had baptized him. I stayed in contact with him and his family as he grew up. He now was in a serious relationship with a woman. They discovered they might be pregnant. He called because she was considering an abortion, something he vehemently opposed.

As we talked I found myself (given my own negative feelings about abortion) asking him: "John, what if she goes ahead and has the abortion? What are you going to do?" (thinking that this action of hers would be so repulsive to him that he would break off the relationship).

"What do you mean, Mike?" he responded. "What are you saying?"

Unwilling to come out and say what I was thinking (and expecting from him), I said: "Well, John, if she has this abortion, how will it affect your relationship in the future?"

"Mike, I love her unconditionally. No matter what she does I will never stop loving her. I just can't not love her."

Never before in my life did I receive such an insight into the depth of Paul's words in Romans: "God proves his love for us in that while we still were sinners Christ died for us" (Rom. 5:8). In its own way this is repeated in the Letter to Titus: "But when the goodness and loving kindness of God our Savior appeared, he saved us, not because of any works of righteousness that we had done, but according to his mercy, through the water of rebirth and renewal by the Holy Spirit" (Titus 3:4–5).

Truly, such love *changes everything*. When it is expressed in such unconditional ways, "nothing in the world will ever be the same."

Creating Relationships That Nurture Love

Because love is a form of energy it must be cultivated to keep on growing. Its pruning comes when we free ourselves from those overpowering forces, often communicated to us in the name of love, which did any-thing but reveal love to us. Love is something given us by our "I am." At the same time it is something that must be nurtured by practice.

In his classic *The Art of Loving* Erich Fromm shows how easily false notions about "love" have become controlling obstacles that keep us from expressing love as a power for good toward others and our world. The problem begins when we see love as connected to being loved rather than loving. As a result we try to become love-able, often in self-destructive ways. Another problem is our notion of love as an object insofar as it is something we "fall into," often at first sight. Rather, Fromm insists, love is an inner energy, an art that must be nurtured; it is a power that must be cultivated in an environment of care, freedom, and trust. Consequently, love is all about building positive and constructive relationships.

In 1991 I joined other brothers in my community to create an atmos-phere that would nurture love between us insofar as we would commit ourselves to a process of ongoing and mutual affirmation and correction.

Because I have wanted to live simply, there was a ten-year period when I didn't have a car, between 1993 and 2003. The other three men with whom I lived at that time each had his own car. Consequently, I had to ask for their cars anytime I wanted to go someplace distant. Two of them had given me the keys for their cars, but the third one assumed I would always ask him and then get the keys. While I found this somewhat controlling on his part, I did not let it become my "problem," as noted earlier. It was just the way things were.

One day, after getting his keys, I forgot to return them to the usual place on the desk in his room. Instead of asking directly for them I found a note on a bulletin board near the kitchen. It was addressed to me. It said, "Mike: Need the keys to my car." At that I blew up.

Following my personality style (as well as my ancestry, I am told), rather than correcting him immediately, as he had done to me, I stuffed my anger by saying nothing and hoping he would feel it instead. But he didn't catch on to my passive-aggressive behavior the next day.

Continuing my negative anger and resentment, I found myself driv-ing with him and another housemate to Appleton, about two hours away. There we listened to Barbara Fiand talk about the difference be-tween groups that are mere organizations (*gesellschaft*) and those that are empowering for the members (*gemeinschaft*).[9] She noted that, since all relationships find us connected to everyone, whether or not those relationships are defined by positive or negative dynamics can have re-sults like the butterfly in Singapore affecting the weather in Appleton.

She noted that all our relationships serve as a constructive or destructive force, not only in themselves, but in their connectedness to the universe itself. At that, I said to myself, "Oh my God! I'm destroying the universe!" Even though it may sound crazy, in a very real way, I believed her then and believe it even more now.

The next morning I said to my colleague: "I was really pissed off at you about the car, and how you were controlling me with your note about 'needing the keys' to it, especially since you have that extra set." At that he said: "Why didn't you tell me right away? I thought we had made the 'ground rule' to correct each other." I responded: "I didn't know our mutual affirmation was strong enough for me to correct you." Then he said, "I know you love me, and that's why I want to know when I do something that bugs you."

He was not able to say those disarming words to me, "I know you love me," in a vacuum; they were articulating a journey of effort made by both of us in this grouping that found us together that had more than a decade of years under its belt.

Such authentic love becomes a force that proves the wisdom of care: when affirmation and correction ground the relationship, you want to continue in such a commitment; you want to "stick around."

"Where There Is Hatred, Let Me Sow Love"

In the days after September 11, 2001, there was a lot of anger in our rhetoric as a people. We saw ourselves as abused; we needed to defend and protect ourselves; it was imperative that we commit ourselves to eradicating the evil of terrorism. Given my feelings of alienation from the rhetoric of resentment and retaliation that seemed to dominate story after story in the newspapers in the days after, I was struck by a little 3 by 5–inch ad placed by my group, the Midwest Capuchin Franciscans, in the *Milwaukee Journal Sentinel*. It was the prayer attributed to our founder, commonly known as "The Prayer of St. Francis." It offered another way of dealing with the hate so many had found rising up within them. It invoked that Source of All Power and Energy in our world, that power that empowers us at all levels:

> Make me an instrument of your peace. Where there is hatred, let me sow love. Where there is injury, pardon; where there is doubt, faith; where there is despair, hope; where there is darkness, light and where there is sadness, joy. Grant that I may never seek so much to be consoled as to console, to be understood as to understand,

to be loved as to love. For it is in pardoning that we are pardoned; it is in giving that we receive, and it is in dying that we're born to eternal life.[10]

The "Canticle of Love" as a Commitment Not Just for Newlyweds

You can hardly ever go to a wedding these days, I am finding, without hearing read the famous "Canticle of Love." "Love is patient, love is kind..." are phrases that have been etched into our psychic memories. However, in light of our Power Chart, it becomes clear that in the taxonomy of love described in the Canticle, love demands the total relinquishment and abandonment of anything that will find us relating to others from attitudes defined by dynamics on the top line. Instead it embraces almost all the elements on the bottom part of the chart. Thus, rather than repeating the Canticle here, we can say what it "is not" and what "it is." In the process we will discover what negative energies will undermine love and which ones will nurture it:

Love Is Not	Love Is
Possessive	Slow to lose patience
Anxious to impress	Constructive
Inflated with self-importance	Good mannered
Seeking self-advantage	That which rejoices over good
Touchy	Enduring
Keeping account of evil	Trustful[11]

A deeper investigation of what love is and is not finds its practitioners "other-oriented" rather than self-centered. In the process the "two become one." Its adherents are set apart radically from our society of individualism; instead they are concentrated on community.

Such were the thoughts I shared at the wedding of a cousin of mine shortly before I began writing this book. I recalled being at gatherings of others involved in the same work as I was. We had come together because we were frustrated by our inability (powerlessness) regarding problems in collaborating with our leader. So we asked a counselor to help us understand our situation of growing alienation and what we could do to get closer to him.

The therapist drew two circles, putting our names in one circle and the leader's name in the other. He said: "The only way you will find common ground with each other will be when you give up your separate interests and work together for some goal. In the process you will find your two separate circles getting closer and closer until they become one." Two days later, I was at the wedding of this couple. There they had proclaimed the "Canticle of Love." I shared with them the therapist's words of wisdom and gave them a wedding card with the two rings merging into one.

Are We "Wired" for Love?

This chapter began with a reference to neuroscientists at the University College of London who have begun researching if there may be a "brain wave that's known as love."[12] Their work and that of neurochemists is revealing that what appears to be self-centeredness in our genes actually is ordered to the survival of our species. This empowers us toward a love that puts us on a path of transcendence. Like it or not, Robert Wright, author of *The Moral Animal*, argues, love is physically mediated. He explains how we are wired for love in a way that compels us to go beyond our self- and group-interests to care for the other in a fascinating example:

> Suppose you are a parent and you (a) watch someone else's toddler misbehave and then (b) watch your own toddler do the same. Your predicted reactions, respectively, are (a) "What a brat!" and (b) "That's what happens when she skips her nap."
>
> Now (b) is often a correct explanation, whereas (a) — the "brat" reaction — isn't even an explanation. Thus does love lead to truth. So too when a parent sees her child show off and senses that the grandstanding is grounded in insecurity. That's an often valid explanation — unlike say, "My neighbor's kid is such a show-off" — and brings insight into human nature.
>
> Yes, yes, love can warp your perception, too. Still, there is an apprehension of the other — and empathetic understanding — that is at least humanly possible, and it would never have gotten off the ground had love not emerged on this planet as a direct result of Darwinian logic.

In a wonderful twist on this "wiring for love," Wright goes on to show that, although it appears to be self- and group-centered, this way of love actually invites us to ever widening circles of care, empathy, and love. He concludes that, even though our child may not be so "special" after all,

...this doesn't have to mean she's not worthy of your love. It could mean instead that other people's kids *are* worthy of your love. But it has to mean one or the other. And — especially given that love can bring truth — isn't it better to expand love's scope than to narrow it?...

Transcending the arbitrary narrowness of our empathy isn't guaranteed by nature. (Why do you think they call it transcendence?) But nature has given us the tools — not just the empathy, but the brains to figure out how evolution works, and thus to see that narrowness is arbitrary.

So evolution has led to something outside itself — to the brink of a larger, more widely illuminating love, maybe even to a glimpse of moral truth. What's not to like?[13]

When we bring a deeper mindfulness to what may or may not be something that actually is in our genes as the reason why we love, all the more we are invited to live lives of love for those around us — in ever widening circles of care. "Let us not tire of proclaiming love," Oscar Romero insisted: "It is the only force that will overcome the world."[14] Indeed, if love is a power and if that power constitutes one of our core energies as individuals and, indeed may even be the basic wiring that constitutes the way we are created for relationships, love becomes the way individuals collectively can move the world into the goal of all power: a way of compassion.

Chapter Seventeen

Universal Compassion: The Consequence of a Commitment to Care

Where I live in Milwaukee, six days a week we have a meal for those who come, appropriately called "Loaves and Fishes." The name recalls not only the reason for the feeding of thousands of people by Jesus and his followers but the reason why it occurred: because of a heart "moved with compassion" (Matt. 14:14; 15:32).

Quite some years ago, while he was in the U.S. Marines, Tom Doyle discovered Milwaukee. Unfortunately, he also struggled with alcoholism. After leaving the Marines, refusing help at the Veterans Hospital for his disease, and frequently not finding work, he used to sleep on one of our porches after coming to our meal for dinner. In 2000 he was murdered. Since then his family has tried to find ways to raise people's awareness of alcoholism as a disease and not a "choice." In response to their efforts with regard to alcoholism and their efforts to fund the meal, my housemate, Capuchin Brother David Schwab, was reported as saying: "I have been very impressed by the level of the Doyles' commitment to help homeless people because of their experience with Tom. Despite the tragic circumstances . . . when you put a face to homelessness and hunger, it translates into real compassion for those in need."[1]

Compassion is the compass we use in the process of finding ourselves consciously connected with everyone and everything in the world, especially those who are most marginalized and in need. Compassion is the power and force of love released, without exceptions or boundaries, into our universe. It is empowering care made universal. It consists of the effort to address the wrongs around us in ever widening circles of justice and mercy to embrace the world with such a kind of care that we work not only to alleviate its pains; we also try to empower those who have been violated in such a way that they can walk free in the future.

While compassion represents a care that becomes increasingly global, I find it well described in the thoughts of Eileen Egan regarding her way of using it to overcome all negative attitudes toward the man who robbed her, leaving her with lacerations to her head, a broken hip, and seven ruptured ribs: "Compassion swallows up all the other emotions," she said. "I looked at my attacker as a human being — a limited [i.e., needy] human being. I don't want to push him further down. I'd rather raise him up, so he can take care of himself."[2]

Compassion: The Consequence of Living a Life of Genuine Care

As David Schwab said, "when you put a face to homelessness and hunger, it translates into real compassion for those in need." I have also found that the deeper we move into the dynamics of the Power Chart our care grows exponentially. In fact, we begin to develop compassion, both proximate and beyond, in ways that the face of one person becomes the face of everyone and everything.

Nel Noddings writes: "We find ourselves at the center of concentric circles of caring."[3] As such we find ourselves engaged with others in varying degrees of caring. These are best defined by the dynamics of "caring about" and "caring for": the further removed personally and proximately from us the more our care will be "about" others' situations. The closer the other comes into our center of influence, the more we will find ourselves caring "for" them. In describing the rippling circles of care she writes:

> In the inner, intimate circle, we care because we love. In particularly trying situations we may act out of ethical sense even here. After all, sometimes we are tired, the other has behaved abominably, and our love is frayed. Then we remind ourselves of the other's location in our system of circles: he is (was) my friend; she is my child; he is my father. The engrossment remains, although its color changes, and we may vacillate between the once natural caring for others to growing concern for ourselves.
>
> As we move outward in the circle, we encounter those for whom we have personal regard. Here, as in the more intimate circles, we are guided in what we do by at least three considerations: how we feel, what the other expects of us, and what the situational relationship requires of us....

Beyond the circles of proximate others are those I have not yet encountered. Some of these are linked to the inner circle by personal or formal relations. Out there is a young man who will be my daughter's husband; I am prepared to acknowledge the transitivity of my love. He enters my life with potential love. Out there, also, are future students; they are linked formally to those I already care for and they, too, enter my life potentially cared-for. Chains of caring are established, some linking unknown individuals to those already anchored in the inner circles and some forming whole new circles of potential caring. I am "prepared to care" through recognition of these chains.

But what of the stranger, one who comes to me without the bonds established in my chains of caring. Is there any sense in which I can be prepared to care for him? I can remain receptive.[4]

Noddings's notion of receptivity invites us to reconsider the teachings of Jesus about care or love of neighbor in the way we move from care for kith and kin to include in our circle of compassion the one normally defined as "enemy."

At the time of Jesus, societies in his Mediterranean world were structured around honor/shame relationships that divided people into "us" and "them," those inside and those outside, family, friends, and enemies. These dynamics revealed three kinds of reciprocity. *General* reciprocity involved the giving of self with no expectation of return, *balanced* forms expected returns, and negative *reciprocity* — ordered toward one's enemies — meant doing to others what you would not want them to do to you. This was reserved to those beyond the immediate and extended household of one's kin and kith — for one's enemies, the outsiders. However, when Jesus said that his followers should love their enemies and pray for their persecutors *so that* they would evidence themselves as members of one family, he was, in effect, saying all reciprocity should be *general*: all people should be seen as one's kin.

A good example of the challenge of this kind of receptiveness and reciprocity in terms of Noddings's notion of proximity occurred while I was finishing this book. The Virginia Tech shooting took place, which killed thirty-two people. This represented the worst campus tragedy in the history of the nation. At the same time, in Iraq and Afghanistan, U.S. soldiers were killed, as they had been almost daily since the beginning of those conflicts. However, the U.S. flags were ordered to be flown at half-staff only because of the Virginia Tech deaths, not because of those in Iraq or Afghanistan. An Army sergeant, Jim Wilt, lamented the disparity.

He wrote that the deaths of U.S. service members were just as violent as those at the university, but they lack the "shock factor of the Virginia massacre." He stated: "If the flags on our [operating bases] were lowered for just one day after the death of a service member, it would show the people who knew the person that society cared, the American people cared."[5]

The Objects of Compassion

Compassion has four levels of concern: for ourselves, for each other, for the least among us, and, finally, for everyone and everything in the universe itself, that is, "universal compassion." This concern arises from a sense of suffering; it is expressed in the effort to free the object of the concern from the suffering. It is care kissing justice — for all.

Compassion for the self, the Buddhists will tell us, invites us to investigate those ways that we allow ourselves to suffer, thus doing violence to ourselves. Many, if not all of these, flow from disordered desires. The source of inordinate desire is found in our needs, both basic human needs and "wants" that have been transformed into needs.

When I was a young adult, I remember reading *Siddhartha* by Hermann Hesse, a novel about a young man's search for ultimate reality which paralleled the journey of the Buddha. I must confess I did not understand his journey — probably because I could not comprehend what had originally made him dissatisfied with his life and surroundings; I had not reached that level of being a "beginner." It took me years to come to this point. Siddhartha Gautama realized that our suffering arises from being enslaved to our desires; the goal of a compassionate life — toward self and others — can be found only in a kind of mindfulness that makes us conscious of the debilitating consequences of being defined by our desires. Mindfulness will not extinguish our desires, but it will help us find a way to change the way our "I am" relates to our desires. When we have found this way, we have found compassion — in ourselves, in our "I am."

Compassion toward others is best expressed in the unconditional love that so many parents learn to show their children. The parent-child bond creates an immediate impulse in the parents to want to alleviate the suffering of the children. This is the drive that impels them to stay up all night when the baby is colicky, for example. It continues when the child has an automobile accident and the parents drop everything to be at the child's bedside. It remains even when a child does something terrible.

This unconditional love gets expressed in the common saying: "S/he's mine, no matter what."

A deeper form of compassion is found when we go beyond care for ourselves and those of our own circle to circles beyond us, especially those of the stranger and, most critically, our enemies. Thus the famous story of Jesus about the Good Samaritan whose heart was moved with compassion at the suffering of one found by the roadside. As the term "compassion to the stranger" implies, one who is suffering estrangement is brought into the circle of one's care with all the healing of the suffering that this may entail.

A final kind of compassion finds us wanting to alleviate pain for all people and all things on the planet and, ultimately, the universe. It is reflected in a desire to be free from any form of control, conflict, or violence toward anyone or anything, as the wonderful insight of Shug in Alice Walker's *The Color Purple* puts it so eloquently: "I knew that if I cut a tree, my arm would bleed."[6]

The Components of a Compassionate Life

In the United States since the late 1990s it has become increasingly difficult to know exactly what is meant by "compassion," especially when it became part of the political rhetoric that helped propel George W. Bush to the White House. I remember his first Inaugural Address where he eloquently spoke of our need as a people to identify ourselves with the Good Samaritan, whose care made a friend of an enemy. I was moved when he addressed the National Religious Broadcasters in Nashville in 2003 and called for a rallying of "the armies of compassion so that we can change America one heart, one soul at a time." However, in reality the political rhetoric played against a background of more people coming to our meal program and other poverty centers as the rich got richer and most of the poor stayed poor. Such rhetoric regarding "compassionate conservatism" often came to mean something like the title of an op-ed piece in the *Wall Street Journal,* "The Imperialism of Compassion."

Beyond political rhetoric and jeremiads about showing too much care for those in developing nations, we need to investigate the components of what authentic compassion invites us to become. Why is this so critical? Simply stated, I believe compassion is the call of all authentic living and the consequence of the unrestricted release of positive power in our world and universe.

Throughout the centuries compassion has been acknowledged as the force that constitutes the core of a truly integrated life. It was the aim of the teaching of the Buddha and the preaching of the Christ. It defines effective counseling (i.e., "unconditional positive regard"), alternative living, as well as cosmic consciousness. Building on our Power Chart, we can say compassion is not just empowered love; it functions as a protest to whatever negative, overpowering, and de-energizing dynamics exist in a situation. Indeed, it works to overcome these negative forces at all levels of life so that those in need as a result of such dynamics of control will themselves be empowered to be free of such violence and be able to freely say "I am" in their own unique way.

Compassion involves three dimensions: observing, or "seeing," judging, or "caring," and acting, or making a commitment to do something about what has been perceived to be wrong.

The first element of compassion constitutes a way of seeing the plight of others around us. Dr. Michael Cavanagh calls this the "cognitive" element. It involves a certain way of perceiving and comprehending another's situation of need. Recognizing the plight of those who are poor and marginalized makes us aware that something is wrong about this. We try to find out what dynamics about the person's life and background, social setting and environment are keeping this person in such negative situations.

The second step in compassion is what Cavanagh calls the "affective" element. This is the "care" that generates the bottom line of our Power Chart. The Christian scriptures call this form of care "a heart moved by compassion" (as in the stories of the "Good Samaritan" and the father who forgives the prodigal son). This compassion rejects the situation in step one, seen as some lack which has brought about the pain. It feels compelled to do something about alleviating the situation.

The third and final step of compassion involves the effort to act in such a way that the plight of the ones in need will be alleviated and kept from happening again. This is what Cavanagh calls the "behavioral" component. It "means responding to another in a way that is helpful."[7]

Cavanagh finds that there are three ways the compassion's triadic elements of seeing, caring, and acting are expressed. Since compassion is a form of power, it can be exercised destructively or constructively. In this context he sees another way the power called compassion is exercised in a kind of "pseudo-compassion." Thus the "imperialism of compassion."

Pseudo-compassion is conditional, and precisely because it is grounded in the conditional, it will be grounded in controlling dynamics as well. When this defines the relationship, the "helper" will continue to do so "until," "but," "except," "when," "only if," etc., etc. In such a situation the one being helped is in reality being used for the helper's goals. He or she is objectified, a means to the ends of the other.

Destructive forms of compassion are overpowering to the one in need. The one experiencing the other's care feels emotionally suffocated and de-energized. It is also destructive when the caregivers become "professional compassion-givers." While they continually extend help to others, they never permit others to show them compassion in their need. We see another destructive form of compassion in the person who is very willing to help out the other but never lets the other forget it. This is a form of paternalism, not compassion.

Constructive compassion, building on all the dynamics we have seen on the bottom line of our Power Chart, may have to be practiced in "tough love" at times. Nevertheless, its goal is the unconditional welfare of the one in need. In other words, the one showing authentic compassion has found a way to *empathize* with or "get into the reality" of the one in need. According to Cavanagh: "Authentic compassion means that, as much as humanly possible, one person sees with the eyes of another, hears with the ears of another, feels with the heart of another." As a result of this sharing of experience, a compassionate person reaches out to do everything possible to share in another's happiness, clarify confusion, or alleviate distress.

Obviously," Cavanagh concludes, "there can be no such entity as perfect compassion, because people have psychological borders that cannot be completely transversed."[8]

Removing the Obstacles
to Authentic Compassion

If the three main components of compassion involve a way of (1) seeing that moves us to (2) care in a way that (3) seeks to empower those beyond us who are in need, how do we — as individuals, as groups, and as a people — a cultivate a compassionate heart? As with the embrace of any good, it involves removing the obstacles that get in the way of that good. Consequently, we need to examine each of the three areas involved in developing compassion to discover the blockages to its realization.

We may ask: Why, in the midst of so much pain on our planet, are so many people unmoved by it? I think it is not so much a matter of ill will but of poor eyesight. They just don't see the pain around them. Why? This blindness comes from a host of sources. Individually, it can come from a lack of awareness generated by being overly concerned with one's own issues and problems. More negatively it can come from self-centeredness and other forms of narcissism that make us the center of our world. As we have seen, it also comes from an isolating indifference.

Sometimes our lack of perception comes from being part of privileged groups. As a result we will easily be seduced into collective unconsciousness and isolation from the victims of unjust social arrangements. Ideologically, we will be negatively impacted by our biases and prejudices. Only when we allow ourselves to be impacted by the victims of those dynamics that benefit us will we begin to "see." Otherwise we will find ways individually, communally, and collectively to inoculate ourselves from their plight. We can become psychically deaf and blind.

Moving to the second level of compassion, we can ask: What if we do begin to "see"? What keeps us from showing care? If our Power Chart is right, we need look no further here (nor when we think of obstacles to "seeing") than to forms of fear. Seeing the pain around me, I might begin to feel responsible as a fellow human being or member of the human race. However, fear will keep me from caring. I will not want to risk getting involved. Another obstacle will be our "compassion fatigue."

Finally, we find that, even though we might "see" and "care" about the suffering occurring among and around us, we often become immobilized or refuse to do anything about it. Why? Fear, again, can be a big motivator. If I try to do something to alleviate the pain of others, it might mean I have to address issues of social justice that explain their plight. This might alienate me from those of my background or lifestyle who have previously "aided and abetted" me as I did the same with them. Another fear arises when we conclude that the problems are too vast and, if I do get involved, nothing good can come from my efforts or they will be futile. I fear failure. However, if I do find others who think the same way, I might be able to get the courage to act, given their supportive care and equal commitment to try to make a difference. We can also find inspiration from the oft-quoted statement of the anthropologist Margaret Mead: "Never doubt that a small group of thoughtful, committed citizens can change the world. Indeed, it is the only thing that ever has."

With this kind of hope that compassion can move our world from indifference to make all the difference in the world we come to our final thoughts. They bring us to the conclusion of our journey through the Power Chart. On the way we learned that control, unchecked, can lead through conflict and violence to breaks, hate, and, ultimately, indifference. They bring us now to that kind of universal care we call compassion.

The Goal of Compassion:
Universal Care for All in the Universe

Ever since I was confronted by members of my Province about my abusive ways of relating, I have had to try to change my way of relating to them and, I guess I would have to say, to everyone else in the process.

The incident occurred at a reconciliation service attended by more than two hundred of us. I had been in the Province almost twenty years and had been in leadership as well. When we were invited to seek out other members in order to be reconciled through repentance or forgiveness, I don't know how many brothers came to me saying something like: "Mike, I need to be reconciled with you," or "Crosby, I need to forgive you." Not a single one came to me to seek to repent. It was totally the other way.

The realization that I had hurt so many others was not easy to accept. However, in my effort to bring about change in the U.S. reality, in the Roman Church, and in the Province itself, I had been perceived as manipulative and dominating, and, therefore, abusive. This reality demanded either denial on my part or an admission of the fact and an acknowledgment that any "problem" I had with others began with myself.

For over twenty-five years I have been on the journey of moving from control to compassion with varying degrees of success. On the one hand, I have fewer people saying things like: "He's really into control," or "You can't tell Michael Crosby anything," or "He really intimidates me." On the other hand, I hear things like: "He's not so bad." "He really does care about what you think," or "He's really trying to change." I am not disheartened that nobody has yet called me "meek and humble of heart," but I do take heart in the fact that, following the words of Jesus, I have come to embrace his way, I am learning his way of discipleship, and I am trying to take his yoke upon my shoulders as I try to lift other less-caring yokes from those around me (see Matt. 11:28–30).

I also am very thankful that, during almost this whole time I have been helped in this effort by two things: living among people who are poor and marginalized and living with brothers who are committed to relate to each other according to the principles of affirmation and correction, as I have outlined. This has helped me become a more caring person, using my power in ways that will move me, others, and the structures of society itself away from the negative dynamics. In the process I am discovering, ever so gradually, the wisdom of words attributed to Albert Einstein with which I want to conclude this book. I identify with him as he declares:

A human being is part of the whole called by us universe, a part limited in time and space. We experience ourselves, our thoughts, and feelings as something separate from the rest. A kind of optical delusion of consciousness. This delusion is a kind of prison for us, restricting us to our personal desires and to affection for a few persons nearest to us. Our task must be to free ourselves from the prison by widening our circle of compassion to embrace all living creatures and the whole of nature in its beauty. We shall require a substantially new manner of thinking if humankind is to survive.

Truly, recalling and believing in the opening words of Jesus in Mark's Gospel about our need to change our hearts for the inbreaking of God's reign or power (Mark 1:15), it is now within the power of all of us to develop this "substantially new manner of thinking." We are Spirit-called not only so that humankind and, indeed, our planet itself, might "survive"; because of the Trinitarian Spirit empowering us, it now is a divinely ordained task to make sure that God's triune power may become the ground for all relationships at all levels of our world as it is in heaven. When this happens the circle of compassion will encircle us all.

Notes

Preface

1. Michel Foucault, "Truth and Power," in *Power/Knowledge: Selected Interviews and Other Writings, 1972–1977,* ed. Colin Gordon (New York: Pantheon, 1980), 119.

2. Gallup Poll, "Does the U.S. Need to Be No. 1?" *Cleveland Plain Dealer,* Forum, March 17, 2007.

Chapter 1 / Power as the Force of Energy at the Heart of All That Is

1. Edward O. Wilson, "Talking about Tomorrow," interview with Thomas Petzinger Jr., *Wall Street Journal,* January 1, 2000, R16.

2. Anthony Giddens, *New Rules of Sociological Method: A Positive Critique of Interpretative Sociologies,* 2nd ed. (Stanford, Calif.: Stanford University Press, 1993), 118.

3. Ibid., 59.

4. Sharon Begley, "The Magical Behavior of Subatomic Particles Moves into Real World," *Wall Street Journal,* January 6, 2006, A9.

5. See Ephesians 1:3–23 and Colossians 1:15–20. More on the Franciscan notion of the primacy of Christ, which is founded in these two passages, will be found in Michael H. Crosby, *Finding Francis, Following Christ* (Maryknoll, N.Y.: Orbis, 2007), 110–12.

6. Nel Noddings insists that "feeling, thinking, and behaving as one-caring mark ethical behavior" itself. Nel Noddings, *Caring: A Feminine Approach to Ethics and Moral Education* (Berkeley: University of California Press, 1984), 117.

7. Nel Noddings, *Women and Evil* (Berkeley: University of California Press, 1989), 186.

8. Nel Noddings, *Starting at Home: Caring and Social Policy* (Berkeley: University of California Press, 2002), 39–49, 52.

9. Sue Monk Kidd, "Birthing Compassion," *Weavings* 5, no. 6 (1990): 26.

10. Hannah Arendt, *On Violence* (San Diego: Harcourt Brace, 1970), 44.

11. Gershen Kaufman, Ph.D., and Lev Raphael, Ph.D., *Dynamics of Power: Fighting Shame and Building Self-Esteem,* rev. 2nd ed. (Rochester, Vt.: Schenkman Books, 1991), 15.

12. Nel Noddings, *Caring,* 49.

13. James Kelly and Scott Nadler, "Leading from Below," *Wall Street Journal,* March 3, 2007, R4.

14. "The biggest threat to America and its values today is not communism, authoritarianism or Islamism. It's petrolism. Petrolism is my term for the corrupting, antidemocratic governing practices — in oil states from Russia to Nigeria and Iran — that result from a long run of $60-a-barrel oil. Petrolism is the politics of using oil

income to buy off one's citizens with subsides and government jobs, using oil and gas exports to intimidate or buy off one's enemies, and using oil profits to build up one's internal security forces and arm to keep oneself ensconced in power — without any transparency or checks and balances." Thomas L. Friedman, "The New Red, White and Blue," *New York Times,* January 6, 2006, A23.

15. Sandra Hack Polaski, *Paul and the Discourse of Power,* Biblical Seminar 62 (Sheffield, U.K.: Sheffield Academic Press, 1999), 21. Polaski's insights, research, and quotations have been very helpful to me in the writing of this book.

16. Anthony Giddens, *Central Problems in Social Theory* (London: Macmillan, 1979), 6.

Chapter 2 / God's Power at the Heart of the World

1. Bruce J. Malina, *The New Testament World: Insights from Cultural Anthropology* (Atlanta: John Knox, 1981), 26–27.

2. I follow the "Two Source" theory of Gospel interpretation: Mark was written first and became the basis for much of what we find in Matthew and Luke. What Matthew and Luke share in common (such as the Beatitudes) came from a second source. What is unique to Matthew and Luke was included because of the authors' conviction of the need for such redactions to address the unique situation of their audiences in the house churches. For more on this, see Pontifical Biblical Commission, "The Interpretation of the Bible in the Church," *Origins* 23 (1994): 497, 499–524.

3. Werner Foerster, *Exestin, exousia, exousiaxo, katexousiaxo,* in Gerhard Kittel, ed., *Theological Dictionary of the New Testament,* trans. Geoffrey W. Bromiley (Grand Rapids: Wm. Eerdmans, 1964), 560.

4. Anne Dawson, *Freedom as Liberating Power: A Socio-Political Reading of the ἐξουσία Texts in the Gospel of Mark* (Freiburg: Universitätsverlag Freiburg, 2000), 11.

5. Ibid., 220.

6. Ibid., 120, 171.

7. The word for power here is *dúnamis.*

8. James M. Reese, O.S.F.S., "How Matthew Portrays the Communication of Christ's Authority," *Biblical Theology Bulletin* 7, no. 3 (July 1977): 140–41.

9. Sandra Hack Polaski, *Paul and the Discourse of Power,* Biblical Seminar 62 (Sheffield, U.K.: Sheffield Academic Press, 1999), 105, 106.

10. Ibid., 106.

11. Sally Purvis, *The Power of the Cross: Foundations for a Christian Feminist Ethic of Community* (Nashville: Abingdon Press, 1993).

12. Polaski, *Paul and the Discourse of Power,* 117.

13. Ibid., 123.

Chapter 3 / The Positive and Negative Constituents of Power

1. Around the same time I wrote these words, the *Wall Street Journal* reported two examples of this phenomenon. One was the U.S. Census Bureau's data showing that, "though the U.S. economy grew robustly in 2004, median household income dipped, median wages fell and poverty rose" (Robert Guy Matthews, "Recovery Bypasses Many Americans," *Wall Street Journal,* August 31, 2005). On the same page another item reported: "The Institute for Policy Studies, a think tank, found

that in 2004, chief executive officers made 431 times as much as the average worker. This up from a 301-to-1 ratio in 2001" ("Study Finds CEO Pay Has Soared since 2001," ibid., A2). In 2003 the average CEO compensation at the large companies jumped 13 percent from 2002. See Gretchen Morgenson, "How to Slow Runaway Executive Pay," *New York Times,* October 25, 2005.

2. Riane Eisler, *The Chalice and the Blade: Our History, Our Future* (New York: Harper & Row, 1988), 80–103.

3. Richard Rhodes, "What Causes Brutality? The People Nurturing It, A Personal View," *New York Times,* October 16, 1999. Rhodes's comments came in support of his well-reviewed *Why They Kill: The Discoveries of a Maverick Criminologist* (New York: Alfred A. Knopf, 1999).

4. Blaine Lee, *The Power Principle: Influence with Honor* (New York: Simon & Schuster, 1997), 52.

Chapter 4 / The Dynamics of Control

1. "Dear Amy," *Los Angeles Times,* April 3, 2007.

2. I believe negative findings related to executives vis-à-vis their workers and parents vis-à-vis their children can have similar dynamics. See "Human Theories of Control: Skilled Incompetence," in Chris Argyris, *Overcoming Organizational Defenses: Facilitating Organizational Learning* (Boston: Allyn and Bacon, 1990), 12–23

3. As I wrote this book it was discovered that, by removing a single gene in mice, they could be turned from fearful creatures into quite daring ones. Benedict Carey, "Timid Mice Made Daring by Removing a Single Gene," *New York Times,* November 18, 2005.

4. Carlos G. Valles, *Let Go of Fear: Tackling Our Worst Emotion* (New York: Triumph Books, 1991), 84.

5. This will be discussed in chap. 9.

6. Greg Hitt, "Fear Is Key as Election Nears: Bush and Kerry Each Portray the Other as Too Great a Risk," *Wall Street Journal,* October 19, 2004.

7. Bob Herbert, "America the Fearful," *New York Times,* May 16, 2006.

8. Robert Frost, quoted in Valles, *Let Go of Fear,* 87.

9. Robert Sheer, quoted in Mielikki Org, "Media: Fear of Looking Unpatriotic Determined Reporting," *San Mateo County Times,* March 20, 2004.

10. Jonathan Clements, "Don't Get Hit by the Pitch: How Advisers Manipulate You," *Wall Street Journal,* January 3, 2007.

11. The book the woman read, which I recommend, was Deepak Chopra, M.D., *Ageless Body, Timeless Mind: The Quantum Alternative to Growing Old* (New York: Harmony Books, 1993). For the questionnaire, see pp. 175–77.

12. "Tools for Handling Control Issues; Eliminating Intimidation"; see online *www.coping.org/control/intimid.htm.*

13. Whitney Bauman, "Terror, Violence, Natality, and Revelation: 'Bowling for Columbine' and *The Culture of Fear,*" *Bulletin for the Council of Societies for the Study of Religion* 33, nos. 3 and 4 (September and November 2004): 77.

14. Joerg Bose, M.D., "On Human Dignity, Lost and Regained," September 8, 2003, speech at the United Nations Fifty-Sixth Annual DPI/NGO Conference, "Human Security and Dignity, Fulfilling the Promise of the Untied Nations." I am

indebted to Rosalind Sanders for the quotations. See "Human Dignity Lost in Midst of Conflict," *Centerings* (Winter 2003): 5.

15. Philip Chard, " 'Control Freaks' Can't Find the Will to Trust," *Milwaukee Journal Sentinel,* September 9, 2003.

Chapter 5 / Why More of Us Are Abusers Than We'd Like to Admit

1. I have adapted this definition from that proffered by two committees of the United States Conference of Catholic Bishops. In their 1992 document on domestic violence, *When I Call for Help: Domestic Violence against Women,* they define abuse as "any kind of behavior that one person uses to control another through fear and intimidation." They note that this "includes emotional and psychological abuse, battering and sexual assault." See Committee on Women in Society and in the Church and the Committee on Marriage and Family Life, National Conference of Catholic Bishops, *When I Call for Help: Domestic Violence against Women, Origins* 22, no. 21 (November 5, 1992): 355.

2. Sigmund Freud, *Civilization and Its Discontents,* trans. James Strachey (New York: W. W. Norton, 1961), 11.

3. Ibid., 89.

4. Ibid., 91.

5. Condoleezza Rice, at a town hall meeting in Paris, February 6, 2005. In Steven R. Weisman, "Secretary Rice, the New Globetrotter," *New York Times,* February 7, 2005.

6. "The Wounds of Words: When Verbal Abuse Is as Scary as Physical Abuse," *Newsweek,* October 12, 1992.

7. As an example of such findings, see Susan Sachs, "Poll Finds Hostility Hardening toward U.S. Policies," *New York Times,* March 17, 2004. Later things began to change. "Shaken by the Iraq war and the rise of anti-American sentiment around the world, Americans are turning inward, a new Pew survey of American opinion leaders and the general public indicates." Meg Bortin, "Survey Finds Deep Discontent with American Foreign Policy," *New York Times,* November 18, 2005.

8. William J. Holstein, "Erasing the Image of the Ugly American," *New York Times,* October 23, 2005. Another example is Jeffrey E. Garten, "Anger Abroad Is Bad for Business," *BusinessWeek,* November 10, 2003, 30.

9. Linda S. McCartney, M.D., "Violence as a Public Health Issue: One Clinician's View," *Park Ridge Center Bulletin* (May–June 2000): 15.

10. Patricia L. Garcia, "State's Social Health Poor, Study Says," *Albuquerque Journal,* November 19, 2003.

11. Linda Starke, ed., *State of the World Annual Report,* Worldwatch Institute (New York: Norton, 2007).

12. "A Dishonourable Practice," *The Economist,* April 14, 2007, 62.

13. For more on this see, "In the Name of Honour," Freedom from Violence Campaign Action Sheet, 1, March 2000, Amnesty International.

14. For more details on the document, see n. 1 above.

15. Bishop Francis Murphy, *Commonweal,* 1992. For further comment on this, see Editorial: "An Adult Church Begins to Stir," *[Canadian] Catholic New Times,* November 6, 2005.

16. Anne Wilson Schaef, *When Society Becomes an Addict* (San Francisco: Harper & Row, 1987), 66, 67.

17. Alice Miller, *For Your Own Good: Hidden Cruelty in Child-Rearing and the Roots of Violence,* trans. Hildegarde and Hunter Hannum (New York: Farrar, Straus, Giroux, 1984).

Chapter 6 / Destructive Dynamics Fueled by Anger

1. William Sloan Coffin, "Be Angry But Do Not Sin: A Spirituality for the Long Haul," *Pax Christi USA* 14(1989): 31.

2. Claudia Wallis, "Does Kindergarten Need Cops?" *Time,* December 15, 2003.

3. Derrick Nunnally, "Raging E-Mails Lead to Big Liberal Award," *Milwaukee Journal Sentinel,* November 12, 2005.

4. Mike McPhate, "Outsourcing Outrage: Indian Call-Center Workers Suffer Abuse," *San Francisco Chronicle,* November 17, 2005.

5. I am indebted for this story about Jerry Sola to an article by Dianne Hales, "Why Are We So Angry?" *Parade Magazine* (September 2001): 10, 12.

6. Jena McGregor, "Sweet Revenge," *BusinessWeek,* January 22, 2007, 68.

7. David Lotto, Ph.D., "The Psychohistory of Vengeance," *Journal of Psychohistory* (Summer 2006).

8. Stephen Juan, Ph.D., "Why Do Humans Seek Revenge," [*Canada*] *National Post,* April 18, 2007.

9. Robert J. Wicks, Psy.D., "A Threat to Christian Communities: Angry People Acting Passive Aggressively," *Human Development* 25, no. 3 (2004): 8.

10. Mary Michael O'Shaughnessy, O.P., *Feelings and Emotions in Christian Living* (New York: Alba House, 1987), 91. I am indebted to O'Shaughnessy for various insights noted in this book.

11. Ibid., 93.

12. Dale R. Olen, *Resolving Conflict: Learning How You Both Can Win and Keep Your Relationship,* A Life Skills Series Book (Germantown, Wisc.: JODA Communications, 1993), 34.

Chapter 7 / Conflict: Its Sources and Debilitating Dynamics

1. Nel Noddings, *Caring: A Feminine Approach to Ethics and Moral Education* (Berkeley: University of California Press, 1984), 55.

2. Dan McCauley, quoted in Jodi Wilgoren, "At Center of Clash, Rowdy Children in Coffee Shops," *New York Times,* November 9, 2005.

3. In the conservative journal *Commentary,* neoconservative writer David Gelernter positively defined "Americanism" as "the set of beliefs that are thought to constitute America's essence and to set it apart; the beliefs that make Americans positive that their nation is superior to all others — morally superior, closer to God." See "Americanism — and Its Enemies," *Commentary* 119, no. 1 (2005): 41.

4. Anthony Giddens, *Central Problems in Social Theory* (London: Macmillan, 1979), 6.

Chapter 8 / Violence in Our Lives, Groups and World

1. Gil Bailie, *Violence Unveiled: Humanity at the Crossroads* (New York: Crossroad, 1995).

2. Robert Hamerton-Kelly has written various articles and books on the subject. See his *Sacred Violence: Paul's Hermeneutic of the Cross* (Minneapolis: Fortress, 1992).

3. Gil Bailie and Richard Rohr teamed up to create *Violence Unveiled: The Gospel at Work in History,* videocassette (Sonoma, Calif.: Florilegia Institute, 1996).

4. Bob Herbert, "Hooked on Violence," *New York Times,* April 26, 2007.

5. David Doege, "Murder by 13-Year-Old Was Inexcusable but Understandable, Lawyer Says," *Milwaukee Journal Sentinel,* August 9, 1999.

6. Peggy Noonan, "The Culture of Death," *Wall Street Journal,* April 22, 1998. When Noonan noted the violence coming from the television set, again, it assumes the television set is in the United States. The difference between the content of television shows in the United States compared to its neighbor, Canada, was noted in "Canadian TV Has Wholesome Appeal," *Detroit News,* January 10, 2002. A seventeen-year study summarized in *Science* in 2002, which tracked seven hundred young people into their adult lives, positively correlated their hours of watching television as minors with acts of "aggression and violent acts as adults": Rosie Miestel, "Adolescents' TV Watching Is Linked to Violent Behavior," *Los Angeles Times,* March 29, 2002.

7. Thomas Merton, *Faith and Violence: Christian Teaching and Christian Practice* (Notre Dame, Ind.: University of Notre Dame Press, 1968), 5–6.

8. William T. Vollmann, *Rising Up and Rising Down: Some Thoughts on Violence, Freedom and Urgent Means,* vol. 1 (San Francisco: McSweeney Books, 2003), 32.

9. Committee on Women in Society and in the Church and the Committee on Marriage and Family Life, National Conference of Catholic Bishops, *When I Call for Help: Domestic Violence against Women,* Origins 22, no. 21 (November 5, 1992): introduction, 353. In the tenth anniversary edition of *When I Call for Help: A Pastoral Response to Domestic Violence against Women,* which was released as "a statement of the U.S. Catholic Bishops" rather than the offering of two committees of the bishops, as was the 1992 document, there are minor but significant changes. They repeat that "violence against women, inside or outside the home, is *never* justified. Violence in any form — physical, sexual, psychological, or verbal — is sinful; often, it is crime as well." But the bishops no longer state that "any kind of behavior that a person uses to control an intimate partner through fear and intimidation" is their definition for abuse. In the 2002 document this is the definition for "domestic violence." In effect, it seems, they have virtually equated abuse and violence. For more on the notion of violence as sinful and sin as violence, see Marjorie Hewitt Suchocki, *The Fall to Violence: Original Sin in Relational Theology* (New York: Continuum, 1994), 45.

10. Vollmann, *Rising Up and Rising Down,* 56.

11. Suchocki, *The Fall to Violence,* 43.

12. "Layoffs Called One of the Biggest Causes of Violent Behavior," *San Francisco Chronicle,* August 16, 1994.

13. Allan Sloan, "The Hit Men," *Newsweek,* February 26, 1996, 44–48. The fact that almost half of the companies featured no longer exist as standing entities themselves indicates that nobody yet has addressed the underlying violence that is inherent in the U.S. brand of corporate capitalism.

14. Pat Robertson, January 5, 2006, quoted in AP release, "Robertson Suggests Stroke Is Divine Rebuke," *New York Times,* January 6, 2006.

15. Patrick Marley, "Mourning, Interrupted: Officials Hope to Block Protests at Soldiers' Funerals," *Milwaukee Journal Sentinel,* January 7, 2006.

16. Tommy Acosta, letter to the editor, "Writer Takes on God the Father," *Sun Lakes Splash,* March 1, 2004.

17. Peggy Noonan, Declarations, "Hatred Begins at Home," *Wall Street Journal,* August 18–19, 2007.

18. Because of space limitations, the chapters on war, hate, and indifference have not been included here. These three chapters can be found on my website under "Spirituality." See *www.michaelcrosby.net.*

Chapter 9 / Recognizing the Need to Change Our Way of Relating in Our Use of Power

1. Dr. Ray Bender, quoted in Martin Hintz, "Crisis or Crossroads?" *M Magazine* 5, no. 12 (2005): 65.

2. Gershen Kaufman, Ph.D., and Lev Raphael, Ph.D., *Dynamics of Power: Fighting Shame and Building Self-Esteem,* rev. 2nd ed. (Rochester, Vt.: Schenkman Books, 1991), 20.

3. Dale R. Olen, *Resolving Conflict: Learning How You Both Can Win and Keep Your Relationship,* A Life Skills Series Book (Germantown, Wisc.: JODA Communications, 1993), 38.

4. Lydia Polgreen, "Youth Power in Liberia: From Bullets to Ballots," *New York Times,* October 29, 2005, A1.

Chapter 10 / The Constituents of Care

1. For more on such examples, see my *Rethinking Celibacy, Reclaiming the Church* (Eugene, Ore.: Wipf and Stock, 2002).

2. Nel Noddings, *Caring: A Feminine Approach to Ethics and Moral Education* (Berkeley: University of California Press, 1984), 117.

3. Richard Rohr, with John Bookser Feister, *Hope against Darkness: The Transforming Vision of Saint Francis in an Age of Anxiety* (Cincinnati: St. Anthony Messenger Press, 2001), 25.

4. Oprah Winfrey, "What I Know for Sure," *O,* April 2001, 232.

5. Gershen Kaufman, Ph.D., and Lev Raphael, Ph.D., *Dynamics of Power: Fighting Shame and Building Self-Esteem,* rev. 2nd ed. (Rochester, Vt.: Schenkman Books, 1991), 140.

6. Eileen Egan quoted in Michael Ryan, "I Refuse to Live in Fear," *Parade Magazine,* October 23, 1994, 73.

7. Noddings, *Caring,* 17, 201. Nel Noddings, *Starting at Home: Caring and Social Policy* (Berkeley: University of California Press, 2002), 52.

8. Noddings, *Caring,* 4.

9. Ibid., 5.

10. Ibid., 23.

11. Blaine Lee, *The Power Principle: Influence with Honor* (New York: Simon & Schuster, 1997), 9–10.

12. Ibid., 3.

13. Robert G. Kegan, *The Evolving Self: Problems and Process in Human Development* (Cambridge, Mass.: Harvard University Press, 1982), 116–20.

14. John Powell, S.J., *Why Am I Afraid to Tell You Who I Am? Insights into Personal Growth* (Allen, Tex.: Thomas More, 1998).

15. Edward Gibbon, by attribution.

16. The *Wall Street Journal* and the Heritage Foundation, a conservative think tank, issue an annual "Index of Economic Freedom" ranking over 150 countries "on such questions as the liberality of trade policy, how much citizens are burdened by taxes and regulation, the soundness of monetary policy, whether property rights are protected, and the size of the black market." These range from the "free" and "mostly free" to the "mostly unfree" and "repressed." Mary Anastasia O'Grady, "The Real Key to Development," *Wall Street Journal,* January 15, 2008. The article has a helpful chart ranking 157 countries on a "2008 Index of Economic Freedom."

17. Jean Vanier, *Becoming Human* (New York: Paulist, 1998), 108.

18. Ben Schott, "Who Do You Think We Are?" Reflections on the General Social Survey of the "American Psyche," *New York Times,* February 25, 2007.

19. Michael W. Foss, *Power Surge: Six Marks of Discipleship for a Changing Church* (Minneapolis: Fortress, 2000), 164.

20. I am indebted for this way of interpreting Robert G. Kegan to Mary Baird Carlsen, *Meaning Making: Therapeutic Processes in Adult Development* (New York: W. W. Norton, 1988), 51.

21. Noddings, *Starting at Home,* 23–24.

22. Robert J. Schreiter, *Reconciliation: Mission and Ministry in a Changing Social Order* (Maryknoll, N.Y.: Orbis, 1992), 34.

Chapter 11 / Signs of Healthy Relationships

1. Synod of Bishops, "Introduction," *Justice in the World,* November 30, 1971, in Joseph Gremillion, *The Gospel of Peace and Justice: Catholic Social Teaching since Pope John* (Maryknoll, N.Y.: Orbis, 1975), 513–14.

2. In the other Synod that took place among the same group of bishops from around the world, in 1971, another allusion was made to the need for conversion on the part of the bishops themselves. In the document *The Ministerial Priesthood* I, 1, they stated: "Impelled by the need to keep in view both the personal and social aspects of the announcement of the Gospel, so that in it an answer may be given to men's most fundamental questions, the Church not only preaches conversion to God to individuals, but also, almost as society's conscience, she speaks as best she can to society itself and performs a prophetic function in this regard, always taking pains to effect her own renewal" (*The Pope Speaks* 16, no. 4 [1972]: 368).

3. *Justice in the World,* nos. 40–44, 522.

4. For more on this, see Nel Noddings, *Starting at Home: Caring and Social Policy* (Berkeley: University of California Press, 2002), 32ff., 53.

5. Jean Stein, Letter to "Metropolitan Diary," *New York Times,* August 29, 2005.

6. Fred Cavaiani, "The Predictability of Caring People," in Counselor's Corner, August 10, 2003.

7. John Pilch, *Wellness: Your Invitation to Full Life* (Minneapolis: Winston Press, 1981), 18.

Chapter 12 / Constructing Relationships That Channel Anger in Positive Ways

1. Carolyn Osiek, R.S.C.J., *Beyond Anger: On Being a Feminist in the Church* (New York and Mahwah, N.J.: Paulist, 1986), 12–13.
2. Thich Nhat Hanh, *Living Buddha, Living Christ* (New York: Riverhead Books, 1995), 14.
3. Mary Jane Ryan, *The Power of Patience* (New York: Broadway Books, 2003).
4. Miriam D. Ukeritis, "Anger on Behalf of Justice," in *Anger: Issues of Emotional Living in an Age of Stress for Clergy and Religious,* Tenth Psychotheological Symposium, ed. Brendan P. Riordan (Whitinsville, Mass.: Affirmation Books, 1985), 134.
5. Ibid., 135.
6. Ibid., 140–41.
7. Kang Kek Ieu, quoted in Seth Mydans, "70's Torturer in Cambodia Now 'Doing God's Work,'" *New York Times,* May 2, 1999.

Chapter 13 / Moving from Conflicts to Collaboration

1. Russell D. Stoeckler, quoted in Annysa Johnson and Felicia Thomas-Lynn, "'I Made a Dumb Mistake,'" *Milwaukee Journal Sentinel,* November 12, 2005.
2. James Carville, "What Makes a Good Husband," *Mirabella* (March/April 1997): 138.
3. Riane Eisler, *The Chalice and the Blade: Our History, Our Future* (New York: Harper & Row, 1988), 7–41, 185–203, passim.
4. Quoted in Jay Solomon, "After the Tsunami, Religious Differences Give Way to Charity," *Wall Street Journal,* January 1, 2005.
5. Richard Conboy, address on collaboration, Midwest Capuchin Franciscans, June 1999.
6. Loughlan Sofield, S.T., and Carroll Juliano, S.H.C.J., *Collaborative Ministry: Skills and Guidelines* (Notre Dame, Ind.: Ave Maria Press, 1987), 26.
7. Ibid., 103.
8. Ibid., 115.
9. Scott Thurm, "Teamwork Raises Everyone's Game: Having Employees Bond Benefits Companies More Than Promoting 'Stars,'" *Wall Street Journal,* November 7, 2005.
10. Ibid., 19.
11. Michael Marigliano, "Friars Gather and Talk about Collaboration," *Re:Cap* 466 (October 6, 2000): 3.
12. Sofield and Juliano, *Collaborative Ministry,* 51.
13. Nel Noddings, *Caring: A Feminine Approach to Ethics and Moral Education* (Berkeley: University of California Press, 1984), 59–60.
14. See CRM: A Customer-Centric Business Strategy, *www.crmguru.com.*
15. Joe B. Tye, "The Paradox of Servant Leadership," *Spark Plug's Monday Spark,* October 31, 2005. For more on Tye's approach to power and leadership, see his website: *www.joetye.com*

Chapter 14 / The Power of Nonviolence

1. Mary Lou Kownacki, O.S.B., "The Doorway to Peace: A Spirituality of Nonviolence," *Pax Christi USA* 17, nos. 1–2 (1992): 28.

2. Mohandas K. Gandhi, quoted in ibid., 29.

3. For more on this approach see Gene Sharp, *Civilian-Based Defense: A Post-Military Weapons System* (Princeton, N.J.: Princeton University Press, 1990). For more on Sharp, see Claire Schaeffer-Duffy, "Honing Nonviolence as a Political Weapon," *National Catholic Reporter,* Paths to Peace Supplement, October 21, 2005, 2a–4a.

4. James H. Forest, *The Ladder of the Beatitudes* (Maryknoll, N.Y.: Orbis, 1999), 48.

5. Blaine Lee, *The Power Principle: Influence with Honor* (New York: Simon & Schuster, 1997), 1–2.

6. Ibid., 128.

7. The expressions of nonviolence noted here owe much to the "Vow of Non-violence" promoted by Pax Christi, the Catholic Peace group. I made this "vow" or commitment in 1999 and have been struggling to be faithful to it ever since, with varying degrees of success.

8. Richard John Neuhaus, "While We're at It," *First Things* 164 (June–July 2006): 71.

9. For more on Pax Christi's "Vow of Nonviolence," see *www.paxchristiusa.org/news_events_move.asp?id=55.*

10. Kathy Long, O.P., "Nonviolence: An Articulation of Criteria," *8th Day Centerings* (Spring 2004): 9.

Chapter 15 / The Recipe for Making Peace

1. Thich Nhat Hanh, *The Sun My Heart* (Berkeley, Calif.: Parallax Press, 1988), 127.

2. St. Francis of Assisi, in *The Legend of the Three Companions,* 35, in Regis J. Armstrong, O.F.M.Cap., J. A. Wayne Hellmann, O.F.M.Conv., and William J. Short, O.F.M., eds., *Francis of Assisi: Early Documents* II (New York: New City Press, 2000), 89.

3. Rachel Emma Silverman, "Making Peace over Money," *Wall Street Journal,* October 21–22, 2006.

4. Rachel Emma Silverman, "How to Keep Peace among Heirs," *Wall Street Journal,* April 18, 2007.

5. Kirk Johnson, "Reaction to Wreath Edict Leads to More Peace Symbols," *New York Times,* November 29, 2006.

6. See Ralph K. White, *Nobody Wanted War: Mispreception in Vietnam and Other Wars* (Garden City, N.Y.: Double Anchor Books, 1970).

7. Karen Grigsby Bates, "Say 'Peace' to a Muslim and Mean It," *Youngstown (Ohio) Vindicator,* September 25, 2001.

8. Mahvish Khan, "To Keep the Peace, Study Peace," *New York Times,* July 27, 2002.

9. Carol Vogel, Inside Art, "A 'Peaceable Kingdom' by Hicks to Be Auctioned," *New York Times,* November 25, 2005.

10. David Wessel, "As Rich-Poor Gap Widens in the U.S., Class Mobility Stalls," *Wall Street Journal,* May 5, 2005.

11. Chris Giles, "UK Equality Gap Widens as Rich Cash in under Brown," *Financial Times,* June 22, 2007.

12. "For Whosoever Hath, to Him Shall Be Given, and He Shall Have More," *The Economist,* August 11, 2007, 36.

13. Clarence Page, Commenting on a *Time* survey: "How Rich Do You Think You Are? Well, Here's the Truth," *Chicago Tribune,* September 19, 2003.

14. Mark D. Naison, "Black Poverty's Human Face," *BusinessWeek,* September 19, 2005.

15. John R. Tennant, "France's Clash of Cultures Was Fated," *San Francisco Chronicle,* November 13, 2005.

16. Vatican News Service, Zenit, September 13, 2005.

17. Michael H. Crosby, "A *Kairos* Movement in the Catholic Church," in "Church Reform" at *www.michaelcrosby.net.*

Chapter 16 / Growing in Love

1. Dan Black and Charles Hart, "Love Changes Everything" (The Really Useful Group, 1992).

2. E. Cary Simonton, in Gerrit Scott Dawson, Marcus Atha, and E. Cary Simonton, "On Our Faces Together," *Weavings* 22, no. 2 (March–April, 2007): 39.

3. Emily Eakin, "Looking for That Brain Wave Called Love," *New York Times,* October 28, 2000.

4. Helen Fisher, referred to in ibid.

5. Pierre Teilhard de Chardin, *On Love and Happiness* (San Francisco: Harper & Row, 1984), 3, 131–32.

6. Brian Sweeney, quoted in "Voices from Above, 'I Love You, Mommy, Good Bye,'" Word for Word Column, *New York Times,* September 16, 2001.

7. Dale R. Olen, Ph.D., *Accepting Yourself: Liking Yourself All of the Time,* a Life-Skills Series Book (Germantown, Wisc.: JODA Communications), 11–12.

8. Ibid., 23.

9. Some of these notions are further developed in Barbara Fiand, *Refocusing the Vision: Religious Life into the Future* (New York: Crossroad, 2001), 117–23.

10. Capuchin Franciscans, Province of St. Joseph, "Peace Prayer of St. Francis," *Milwaukee Journal Sentinel,* September 19, 2001. Although it contains sentiments exhibited in the life of St. Francis of Assisi, this "Prayer" was first circulated in the last century, around the time of the First World War. For more on its origin, see Frieder Schulz, "The So-Called Prayer of St. Francis," trans. Peter J. Colosi, *Greyfriars Review* 10, no. 3 (1996): 237–56.

11. I have chosen to use a contemporary translation of the Canticle of Love found in St. Paul's First Letter to the Corinthians 13:4–8. See J. B. Phillips, *The New Testament in Modern English* (New York: Macmillan, 1960), 361.

12. Eakin, "Looking for That Brain Wave Called Love," *New York Times,* October 28, 2000.

13. Robert Wright, "Why Darwinism Isn't Depressing," *New York Times,* April 21, 2007.

14. Archbishop Oscar Romero, September 25, 1977, in Oscar Romero: *The Violence of Love,* comp. and trans. James R. Brockman, S.J. (San Francisco: Harper & Row, 1988), 9.

Chapter 17 / Universal Compassion

1. David Schwab, O.F.M.Cap., in "Homeless Man's Family Honors His Memory," *Good News: St. Ben's Community Meal* (Winter 2007): 1.

2. Eileen Egan, quoted in Michael Ryan, *The Power of Patience* (New York: Broadway Books, 2003), 23.

3. Nel Noddings, *Caring: A Feminine Approach to Ethics and Moral Education* (Berkeley: University of California Press, 1984), 46.

4. Ibid., 46–47.

5. Sergeant Jim Wilt, quoted in "Sergeant Questions Lowering Flag for Tech," *Milwaukee Journal Sentinel*, April 24, 2007.

6. Alice Walker, *The Color Purple* (New York: Washington Square Press, 1982), 178.

7. Michael E. Cavanagh, "Rediscovering Compassion," *Journal of Religion and Health* 34, no. 4 (1995): 318.

8. Ibid., 321.

Of Related Interest

Thomas Merton
PASSION FOR PEACE
Reflections on War and Nonviolence

Revised edition

Violence, war, and terrorism fill our televisions, newspapers, and websites. To meet the great need for nonviolent wisdom in the tradition of Martin Luther King Jr. and Mahatma Gandhi, Crossroad presents this new and reedited version of Thomas Merton's *Passion for Peace*. The book presents Merton's most important insights into themes such as the nature of violence, armed conflict, Christian responsibility, and the individual in the state.

"Thomas Merton's most important writings on peace and non-violence. Essential Reading."   — *Praying Magazine*

"These writings are, besides being stirring reminders of the Christian duty to prosecute peace, documents of importance to American history as much as or more than to Christian history."   — *American Library Association Booklist*

0-8245-2415-2, paperback

crossroad